VIEW OF THE
LOWLANDS

VIEW OF
THE LOWLANDS

Described and
photographed by

HUBERT FENWICK

ROBERT HALE · LONDON

By the Same Author

Architect Royal
The Châteaux of France
The Auld Alliance
Scotland's Historic Buildings
Scotland's Castles
Scotland's Abbeys and Cathedrals

Robert Hale Limited
Clerkenwell House
Clerkenwell Green
London EC1

ISBN 0 7091 9322 X

Photoset, printed and bound
in Great Britain by
REDWOOD BURN LTD
Trowbridge, Wiltshire

Frontispiece:
The spirit of the Borders: Neidpath Castle on a bend of the Tweed near
Peebles.

CONTENTS

ACKNOWLEDGEMENTS

I should like to express my thanks to Her Majesty Queen Elizabeth the Queen Mother for graciously permitting me to visit her castle at Mey and record it, and to all those who wittingly or unwittingly have contributed to this and other books of mine by entertaining me in their homes, especially my Australian friends at Lochnaw for taking me to Kirkmadrine. I am grateful to Miss Moira Campbell, photo-librarian at the Scottish Tourist Board, for her assistance at various times; to Mrs Mona Bennett for fair-copying my original manuscript; and to Ronald Miller of Pittenweem for letting me stay in his unique and historic priory, for reading my proofs and accompanying me on many of my journeys.

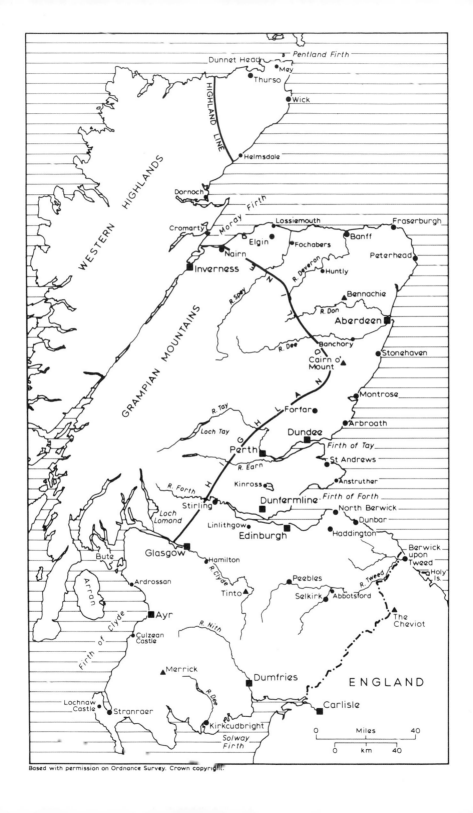

Based with permission on Ordnance Survey. Crown copyright.

ILLUSTRATIONS

INTRODUCTION

OPINIONS DIFFER as to the precise line of demarcation between the Scottish Highlands and Lowlands, if such a division actually exists, which is doubtful. My former employer, Ian Lindsay, believed that the Lowlands marked the limit of Norman penetration, the Highlands representing for them 'Barbaria'. Others recall the use of Northumbrian English throughout the Lowlands, a tongue which was certainly universal from Caithness to Berwickshire in the days of the eleventh-century Queen Margaret and her feudalizing sons. Today, Netherlandish words and sounds are common along the east coast, as Irish ones are in the south-west, but there undoubtedly was a recognizable Lowland speech throughout the area in medieval times, one that clashed completely with the Gaelic spoken in the Highlands. One might say, therefore, that the division is, paradoxically enough when one thinks of the Norman penetration, between Celt and *Sasunnach*, or Saxon, with overlaps and enclaves here and there. From the tip of Caithness to the Moray Firth, with only the mountains of Sutherland intervening, the same language prevailed as in Aberdeenshire, Angus and Fife and right down beyond the Borders. The late Sir Thomas Innes of Learney, Lyon King of Arms, found this out a few years ago when he mistakenly tried, and failed, to foist an alien motto on to the Burgh of Wick, county town of Caithness, the Provost informing him that they did not speak like that in their part of the world! The folk are firmly non-Highland in that northern airt, as are those on the seaward side of the Black Isle: but where is the so-called Highland Line?

Inverness describes itself as 'capital of the Highlands', and the traditional 'Highland Line' is said to be not west of it but somewhere to the east, presumably on the road to Nairn. Yet the fisherfolk of Nairn always spoke 'English', as opposed to Gaelic, so that the River Nairn which divides the town is probably as near to a definite demarcation as we shall find. Coastal Moray, the so-called 'garden of Scotland', is absolutely Lowland, though never out of sight of the Highlands, and this continues through Banff to Buchan, in northern Aberdeenshire, where another triangle of Lowland speech and ways brings one to the 'Granite City' itself. South of Aberdeen the mountains again come closer to the sea before falling back again in Kincardineshire and Angus to run in a south-westerly direction across Perthshire and Stirling until reaching the Firth of Clyde at Dumbarton. Everything south of that may fairly safely be labelled Lowland, though Galloway, in the south-west, is Celtic in origin and feel and was formerly Gaelic-speaking. Still, it is Lowland now and has, since the Middle Ages, been closely associated with Northumbria and the archdiocese of York, to which it was attached almost until the Reformation.

If the division between Highland and Lowland is not so much one between north and south as between east and west, it is also not primarily between plain and hill either, for most of Scotland is hilly, with an average altitude above 2,000 feet. There is, on the other hand, a geological division between the two areas which can often be seen even by passing travellers. A particularly obvious example of this lies on the road north from Perth to Dunkeld, about half-way between the two places, where the softer Lowland pastures actually turn into bumpy Celtic fields, with stones lying around, and marshy lochans and scrub, almost before one's very eyes; behind runs the range of Highland hills stretching at an angle across the country like a natural barrier against the intruder. Although the Highlands have mostly been tamed and Scotland is rather more homogeneous than most people think, there remain differences in geography as well as custom that allow us to distinguish between Highland and Lowland quite legitimately. The Lowlands are the part of the country where three-quarters of the population live, where life is easier and where nature has been developed and controlled for a long period, where the feudal system was fully established by the twelfth century and where in essence conditions were very little different from those in other parts of Britain until first the Plantagenets and then the Tudors thought they would like to make the whole of Scotland part of their domains. It was then that England and Scotland grew apart, the Scots calling in the French to counterbalance English acquisitiveness and forging close commercial and cultural links with the Low Countries and Scandinavia. Scottish culture, which had begun on similar lines to English, then evolved its own special traits and forms; speech altered and taste, and more importantly, Scottish architecture became the splendid and unique thing it is. The Highlands only slowly and partially joined in these developments, being sparsely populated, difficult of access and inward-looking, in the mountains; the western seaboard was for years under the control of the Lords of the Isles and scarcely at all subject to the kings of Scots.

View of the Lowlands is a personal view in words and pictures of the area south and east of the 'Highland Line'. It is not a gazetteer or guide of any kind, and the photographs were taken mostly over the last twenty-five to thirty years, in the course of the author's professional work as architect and historian, not with this book in mind. They cover, albeit not impartially, the Scottish Lowlands, from the view over the Pentland Firth from the battlements of the Queen Mother's home in Caithness to that through Vanbrugh's monumental entrance to the former King's Own Scottish Borderers' Barracks at Berwick; they take in the north-east from Moray to Angus, Fife and the central plain, Edinburgh and Glasgow and include views of Scotland's south-western extremity, Galloway, which is actually south of Durham.

Viewers and readers will no doubt detect a slight architectural bias, which is only natural. I make no apology for this. In humanized landscapes such as the ones described, buildings play a salient role, they denote the presence of people, record their history and tell us how they live. It is in their buildings that folk are remembered long after they themselves have gone, and it is one of the main differences between Highland and Lowland, the amount and type of building. Of course, man also made the countryside, and one has only to look at a garden gone to seed to see what our surroundings would be like if we did not develop and maintain them as Biblically enjoined. Take people out of a view and you have landscape, but take their labours out as well and you have a wilderness. If *View of the Lowlands* occasionally reveals a wilderness, it is only because man has created it either deliberately or by neglect; it is not the natural state, as it is in some of the remoter parts of the Highlands.

The Queen Mother's castle at Mey, Caithness – a view from the roof towards Dunnet Head, the most northerly point on the Scottish mainland.

CHAPTER ONE

THE NORTH-EAST

WHEN I TOLD someone that I was writing a book with the title *View of the Lowlands* and mentioned that I intended to begin with the view from the battlements of Her Majesty the Queen Mother's Caithness home, they said, "Surely that's not in the Lowlands, is it?" In fact it is, or most of Caithness is. The top, flattish triangle between Wick and Thurso is Lowland in speech, geography and history, though it lies immediately opposite Nordic Orkney and north of the mountains of Sutherland; 'beyond the Highlands', in much the same way as Pembroke, 'little England', lies beyond Wales. Miss Sinclair, whose family acquired Barrogill, or the Castle of Mey, in Jacobean times, described it in the early-nineteenth century as possessing the dignity of a Highland residence with the elegance of a house in London. This was after a considerable baronial face-lift and when a new battlemented roof-line had been created shortly after the Napoleonic Wars, when the coast nearby was guarded by batteries against a possible invasion. Dunnet Head, actually the northernmost point of the British mainland, is seen to advantage from the roof of the Castle of Mey against a background of the dangerous swirling waters of the Pentland Firth and, on the other side, the majestic red cliffs of Orkney. There is always a wind, even on the sunniest day; indeed, it is so persistent that Sandy Webster and his wife, who look after the Queen Mother's home and came from Balmoral, nearly gave it up after their first winter, so nerve-wracking did they find it. The climate has its rewards, however, as I am sure the royal lady who restored it quickly found out. There is the clearest of atmospheres and a real Indian summer, in October, when she often goes there, as well as in August for her birthday, when the roses are at their best. Then there is the very fine walled garden in which the trees and shrubs and some surprising things are protected behind tall Caithness slates, in place of hedges. These have paved the streets of Europe in the past, and one is sorry to see them replaced by concrete. Her Majesty also has an almost unique treasure in her small woods, meticulously kept in existence by constant under-planting and originally supported against the wind by raspberry canes.

It was a joiner in Wick whose comments anent buildings and taste generally the Queen Mother quoted when visiting the National Trust for Scotland Headquarters in Edinburgh during European Architecture Heritage Year: "If it looks right, it is right," observed the perspicacious craftsman. One only wishes more folk would take this simple philosophy to heart, as Her Majesty herself obviously does, since her restoration of the Castle of Mey has been a model of its kind, a genuine renovation in which the work of a variety of periods and styles has been retained and adapted, albeit against purist advice, so that the history and age of the place are there for all to see, not tidied up and camouflaged as is so often the case nowadays.

Dounreay atomic plant is not far off, but almost as much benefit has come to Caithness from Her Majesty's presence and patronage as from that enterprise, and Wick airport is a busy one. There is now an attractive hotel at Freswick Bay made out of an ancient manor-house, a tall, somewhat gaunt mansion but typical of the district, not wholly dissimilar from the first state of Barrogill, which began life as a fortified granary of the bishop of Caithness. Wick itself is not especially exciting; respectable and orderly, Lowland to a degree, its inhabitants still speaking that precise form of English which had its beginnings long before Bannockburn or the earlier Norman settlements and which was once the tongue of all but the Celts between the Humber and the Pentland Firth.

South of Wick the Highlands encroach upon the scene, with a few Lowland fishing-villages, some with Norse names, pressing back against the hills to prevent themselves being pushed into the sea. The road hereabouts follows a veritable *corniche*, while the train, spared in the Beeching cuts, is forced to find an inland route before returning to the coast at Helmsdale, in Sutherland. Soon one is at Dunrobin and Golspie, in a different ambience, a different lilt in the speech and different traditions, including the dropping of reserve and speaking to strangers and passers-by. The capital of Sutherland is Dornoch, which quiet little town was the seat of the bishop of Caithness in the Middle Ages and boasts a much restored Norman cathedral and former episcopal palace, or castle, now an hotel. Both were built by Gilbert de Moravia, the first bishop, treasurer to Alexander II of Scots and of the same family from whom the dukes of Atholl and Sutherland descend and which gave its name to the Moray Firth and shire. Of course, most travel in the thirteenth and later centuries was by sea, hence the close contacts along the coast and the distinct and largely unbridged cleavage of peoples and cultures inland. One used to travel north partly by sea and partly by land, across three estuaries, the Firths of Moray, Cromarty and Dornoch, and this was the same route as followed by feudalizing barons and their Church. Today the difficulties of the terrain and the deep indentations made by the sea have been partially overcome by modern roads and two new bridges, with a third projected. The old, terrifying Kessock Ferry between Inverness and the Black Isle has recently been superseded, as it had itself superseded the older ferry between Fort George and Chanonry Point, near Fortrose, the mixture of military and ecclesiastical nomenclature recalling ancient usage. Fortrose was the seat of the bishopric of Ross and retains, in its pleasant rose-hued houses set around a green, the residue of a cathedral close, or chanonry. Fort George was built to restrain the Highlanders from further adventures after

The Black Isle: a view of Cromarty Firth with the hills of Sutherland in the background, and Cromarty left centre.

the failure of the Jacobite rebellion.

Until the contemporary rejuvenation of Inverness and the considerable industrial progress engendered by the oil boom, the Black Isle, really a peninsula, gently decayed, its coastal villages drawing a regular but modest clientele, with a certain amount of fishing, and the red, volcanic soil producing splendid oats that vie with those of Midlothian as making the best porridge in the world. Cromarty, at its easternmost point, lay out on a limb, indeed geographically still does, guarding the curious and dramatically narrow entrance to its wide, safe firth and itself guarded by two huge cliffs, the northern and southern Sutors. It is one of the least spoilt auld Scotch burghs left to us, having been built all of a piece in the eighteenth century by an 'improving' laird, with breweries and rope-works set up to augment declining maritime activities.

The houses are built of the local warm-pink sandstone in a good plain style, well proportioned and complemented by a charmingly domed courthouse and a kirk with a laird's box, or gallery, and amusing bell-cot. Much of the work was provided for Gaelic-speaking immigrants, whose worship was catered for in a separate chapel, today in ruins above the town, not far from the monument to Hugh Miller, rival with Sir Thomas Urquhart as Cromarty's foremost son. Urquhart translated Rabelais into English, while Miller committed suicide in his fifties almost certainly as a result of mental strain consequent upon the conflict in his brain between what he discovered as a geologist and scientist and his strict fundamentalist upbringing. Sir Thomas Urquhart had no such problem; he had his library, his travels and his Cavalier loyalty, and he died of laughter, it is said, on hearing of the restoration of Charles II in 1660.

Cromarty Castle was demolished by the Rosses, who replaced the Urquharts as superiors, or feudal barons, and

Cromarty: a view towards the North Sutor, with the dome of the Court House (bottom left), Hugh Miller's Monument (centre) and a ruined Gaelic chapel.

they built the very fine Adam mansion that stands on the site today. It was designed by Robert Adam's clerk of works in imitation of Culloden House, near Inverness, thought to have been by Adam himself. It is elegant to a degree and has an intriguing back entrance via a tunnel that enters half-way up the hill from the town. Cromarty subsequently fell on evil days but acquired a splendid new lighthouse in Regency style in the early-nineteenth century, one of those erected about this time by the newly formed Northern Lighthouse Commission of which Sir Walter Scott was a Commissioner. The coasts of Scotland and the islands were supplied with many of their existing lights about the same time and most retain their splendidly simple but beautiful architecture, though now throwing across the waves the largest and strongest candle-power available. Chanonry Point also has its Regency light shining out towards Fort George, where the Adam family, *père et fils*, worked – this helping to explain Robert's presence and influence in the region. Henry Mackenzie, author of *The Man of Feeling* and Scott's particular friend, records how as a boy he met the young Robert Adam in his grandfather's house in Nairn and how Adam sketched out a design for a new house, which was not built but, according to Mackenzie, was the first essay of its kind by the future famous architect.

Fort George was meant to cow the Highlanders into good behaviour; it certainly could not do more since it was not built until after the 'Forty-five'. It was strategically placed between Highland Inverness and loyal Lowland districts and was almost within sight of Culloden Moor, on the northern edge of the hills. (I have described it in detail in my *Scotland's Castles* and given its arrow-shaped plan jutting out into the Moray Firth.) It might be said to mark the end of the Highlands and the beginning of the Lowlands as a continuous region, though the division is almost as inconsequential as in parts of Switzerland, where French and German villages, Protestant and Roman Catholic, succeed each other in extraordinarily illogical fashion. Hereabouts the Gaelic tongue no longer dominates, except in place-names, but in Nairn it used

A well-preserved mill in the Laich o'Moray, near Spynie. The so-called 'Garden of Scotland', coastal Moray is fertile and warmed by the last lick of the Gulf Stream.

to prevail, and Samuel Johnson mentions that the town proper was Celtic in feeling and speech while the Seatown, on the east side of the River Nairn, was 'English'. If that river does indeed mark some sort of true demarcation, then Kilravock Castle, which was built by and still belongs to the Norman family of Rose, would be Highland, and Cawdor, which belongs to a Campbell, would be Lowland.

Nairn has a warm and dry climate, one of the best on the Moray Firth and appreciated even by Italians, who used to go there regularly – hence, no doubt, the old-fashioned and somewhat gay bathing-huts that graced the beach. The Moray Firth is renowned for its equableness, its shores being washed by the last lick of the Gulf Stream before it is finally cooled down by the chilly waters of the German Ocean. The 'Laich o'Moray', as the coastal plain is called, is protected

Left: The ruined towers and Chapter House of Elgin Cathedral viewed from the bridge over the Lossie. Right: A close in Elgin, county town of Moray. The burgh has decidedly Lowland characteristics despite the proximity of Highland hills to the south.

from cold winds by mountains to the north and west and is often referred to as 'the garden of Scotland', and although East Lothian also claims that privilege, apricots do not grow there as they do here. The towns along the coast have a certain sameness, which, if not exactly dull, certainly results from rebuilding at more or less the same time, a century or so ago when prosperity followed less peaceful times. Elgin, the capital, might itself seem dull if it were not for its superb cathedral, moving and splendid even in ruin, and a number of old houses with arched lower storeys, the streets being once arcaded all along. They were known as 'piazzas' and were formerly to be seen in other Scottish towns and cities.

Between Nairn and Forres is Brodie Castle, redoubt of the family of that name and recently presented to the National Trust for Scotland with the required endowment, Ninian Brodie himself staying on in part as tenant. It has been harled

since, ostensibly to save expense, repointing and maintenance, but one wonders what Brodie of Brodie thinks of this
and whether, in fact, such ruthless treatment does not defeat
the original aim of preserving intact an ancient and historic
building? It is an old hobbyhorse of mine, attacking unnecess-
ary harling and the disguising of old structures behind a
coating of chippings and Snowcem 'porridge', but I have both
authority and precedent for my comments in the aims and
purpose of the Society for the Protection of Ancient Buildings, founded by William Morris, wherein would-be protec-
tors are advised not to restore but to repair, "to do as little as
possible, otherwise the attributes of old age we admire so
much are irrevocably lost". A good example of this advice
being followed, perhaps even under Morris's aegis, may be
seen at Kellie Castle, in Fife, which Professor Lorimer made
wind- and water-tight and sufficiently habitable without
altering either its appearance or its character. Perhaps that is
why his son, the architect Sir Robert, only harled when struc-
tural alterations demanded it. When he did so, he did it
sympathetically, never taking the harling right down to the
ground, for instance, where it gets all splashed and dirty, but
finishing on a stone plinth; never covering over the crowsteps, but leaving a stone margin, and merging his harling
into the general pattern of the building, not creating a false
contrast as is done so often nowadays. It is unfortunate that
what he and others occasionally did out of necessity has
become a virtue, even a new aesthetic, a false one, beginning
as a device to cover up extraneous breeze blocks and bricks
and ending up as an official form of 'tarting up' – there is no
other word for it.

North of Elgin, towards the sea at Lossiemouth and
Burghead, is that Morayshire garden where the apricots
grow, also Gordonstoun School and Duffus Castle, erstwhile
seat of the Moravias and now tummeldoun in lumps and
bumps around its grassy motte. Spynie, palace of the bishops
of Moray until the early-eighteenth century, is presently
being preserved by the Department of the Environment and

Innes House, Moray, built in 1640 by the Edinburgh master-mason William Aytoun. Note the 'English' park.

should be open to the public before long. It was surrounded by a moat which took the form of a loch, but this is now drained and part of the general agricultural scene, in a landscape of woods, fields and farms, orchards and mills, not to mention handsome country mansions such as Innes House, which was designed by William Aytoun, royal master-mason and principal builder of Heriot's Hospital, the finest Renaissance structure in Edinburgh. It boasts amongst other things tall 'English' chimney-stalks, set diagonally to the gable end, and copied from Tudor and Jacobean examples. Almost in the same year, Coxton Tower, the epitome of an out-of-date Scots laird's eyrie, was erected, on the southern side of the main road leading out of Elgin towards Rothes. Fear and suspicion inspired this remarkable toy tower, perfect in every detail yet created in Caroline times and within a few miles of contemporary Innes House. In a way, the two structures reflect the juxtaposition of Highlands and Lowlands here-abouts, the different temperaments and attitudes to life, for nowhere, even in the warm and verdant Laich o'Moray, is one out of sight of Highland hills, indeed of mountains, which rise up behind, to the south, and in front across in Sutherland.

The Spey is surely a Highland river, flowing into the sea near Kingston, a name recalling Charles II's landing there in 1650 and his being made to sign the Solemn League and Covenant, a nasty document which imposed on the young monarch the obligation to establish strict Presbyterianism not only in Scotland but in the rest of the United Kingdom. The fact that he was not allowed to land at all unless he left Prince Rupert behind also speaks volumes for the characters of those who 'welcomed' the man who subsequently declared "Presbyterianism is no religion for a gentleman" and went down in history as 'The Merry Monarch'.

We are here in fruit-and-vegetable land, with Baxter's canning-factory at Fochabers, a small township whose beautiful central square with fine steeple and classical façades has been ruined by a 'modern' intrusion in one corner. (It seems a losing battle trying to explain to people that façade architecture must not be tampered with, that it is based not on the picturesque or the romantic but on proportion and style, and that any intrusion, even a well designed one in another style, spoils the whole effect.) The dukes of Gordon lived nearby and were responsible for Fochabers' patrician build-ings. Gordon Castle, a Georgian refacing of an older structure and in part the work of an architectural member of the Baxter family, has been mostly demolished to leave a small, original tower and some outbuildings which have been made habit-able.

As one approaches Banffshire, the fruit- and vegetable-culture fades out, but not the distilling, and along the coast fishing takes over importantly. The fishing-villages string out all the way to Fraserburgh and round the corner to Peter-head; indeed many fishermen in eastern Scotland emanate

The auld kirk at Cullen in Banffshire, a collegiate foundation. Cullen House nearby was the manse for its provost and clerks. Note the outside stair to the laird's gallery.

Right: A view over the roofs of Banff in the direction of Macduff, with the entrance to the Deveron between. The neo-Classical steeple was designed by James Adam.

from here, having followed the shoals down to Fife and Berwickshire. They also tend to live in closed communities, with actual 'Closed Brethren' in some places (that is, strict sabbatarian, officially non-drinking Protestants), while in others Roman Catholics predominate. Cullen is Protestant, a seaside resort and the seat of the principal family in the district, the Ogilvy-Grant-Findlaters, descended from Highlanders but settled here in the eighteenth century to become Lowland. They several times enlarged Cullen House, which began life as a manse for clergy established at the small collegiate church alongside. At the Reformation it became the parish church and was enhanced by an elaborate family pew erected for the

Earl of Seafield, a sort of opera-box entered via external stairs, which survive. A Jacobean enlargement of the house was followed by further aggradizements by the Adam family, the bridge over the Cullen burn, with its almost military aspect, being by the great Robert and probably inspired by experiences at Fort George, while the entrance gates by James Adam look quite Italian despite their northern setting.

Banff is no longer a busy fishing-port, that having moved to neighbouring Macduff, and Banff harbour is all but silted up by the waters of the Deveron, which enters the sea nearby. Several attempts have been made to rectify the position, and in the nineteenth century Thomas Telford was called in to do something about improving the harbour and its facilities. The town has, on the other hand, served for the past three hundred years as a miniature capital rather like those provincial centres on the Continent where local big-wigs and their satellites spend the winter and have town houses. This elegant sociability was encouraged and expanded when the Duffs, bankers in Elgin, were ennobled and backed the right horse in 1745, lending money to the government to defeat Bonnie

Prince Charlie. The result was Duff House, a veritable palace on the Italian model but with an antiquated square-keep plan cleverly disguised by William Adam behind Baroque façades. The banker quarrelled with the architect and refused to pay his fees, so Adam stopped work, and the building was never completely finished, though most of it was, to become in the nineteenth century the home of the Duke and Duchess of Fife, the banker's descendant having married the Princess Royal, eldest daughter of Edward VII. Then Banff (once spelt 'Bamff', and the origin of the saying 'Go to Bamff') really did come into its own again, when all those genteel and aristocratic town houses knew their grandest moment.

The dukes of Fife have since gone. During the war their great mansion was used to house prisoners of war, and it has not yet found a new role. I used to stay at the 'Fife Arms', where Mrs Simpson, who always called me 'Professor Fenwick', presided. She was very much of the old school and kept the hotel as it had been in the 'royal' Duke's day, when anglers came up from the south to fish the Deveron and overflowed from Duff House to this one, which had its own large kitchen-garden, comfortable accommodation and white-frilled, black-skirted staff. It remained thus right up to Mrs Simpson's demise, she herself invariably dressing in black velvet in the evening and doing the rounds of the guests and their rooms personally. Opposite, the locals sat in their cars eating fish and chips, or just chips, with transistors turned on loud, the height of social activity in down-town Banff – yes, down-town, for there are two parallel main streets, one above the other. Now the locals have been to Spain; the fish and chips have moved into 'The Fife Arms' – not literally but figuratively, and social life is a bit gayer than it was, though the anglers have gone and so has much else, including the furnishings and 'palm court' ambience in the hotel.

There have been other changes in Banff. One important and significant one is that the little burgh, one of the most distinguished in Scotland, where the 'ding-it-dooners', or demolishers of anything more than fifty years old, really

Banff boasts a go-ahead Preservation Society, one of whose projects was the restoration of this delightful Jacobean town house, until recently a butcher's shop.

began in earnest, has now given birth to a flourishing and forward-looking Preservation Society. It is run entirely by local people, buys old properties that come up for sale, restores them and re-sells. It has been an enormous success, the latest effort being to find a future for Banff Castle, which is too big as a single house and not easily divided; but it will be done. The first dose of 'dinging-doon' woke them up, and in such a hurry that a year or two ago, when I was invited to lecture a second time to them, I saw in my audience the very provost who before had led the demolishers. He is now a converted preservationist! The great thing about a small county town like Banff is that it is far enough away from overpowering neighbours not to be too drawn towards their ideas and fancies and able thereby to sustain a life of its own. It lies about half-way between Inverness and Aberdeen, which is the nearest large city; and Aberdeen itself is far enough away from Edinburgh or London to have its own life, and that despite the 'Oilies' who dominate its economy.

The coast runs on to Fraserburgh, the fishing-villages clinging to the cliffs lining the rocky shore. The inland areas are fertile but bleak in this the easternmost corner of Scotland, with its elbow sticking right out into the North Sea. It has long been occupied and developed, though there are not many trees, and those that exist are bent over with the wind. It was here in Buchan, amongst his own folk, that Lord Forbes of Pitsligo hid for the last years of his life, protected from search-parties by the people whose laird he was. He was a philosopher of international repute, a regular correspondent with others abroad, especially in France, his disputations with the Jansenists being well known, so that it was with some reluctance that he supported the Jacobite cause, which was his undoing, as indeed it was of so many of the gentry in the north-east. Traditions have died slowly in Buchan, and in particular the speech known as the 'Doric', which even to other Scotsmen is almost a different language.

At Fraserburgh is the very first of the Northern Light-houses erected before the turn of the eighteenth century. It was built on top of an old Fraser watch-tower which, with it, has been painted white. It is not unpleasant, however, and certainly better than being harled! Inside is a fifteenth-century chapel retaining ecclesiastical and royal insignia. Fraserburgh is a grey town, while Peterhead, not far south, is all pink granite, famous for it and also as the original home of so many Scottish fishermen's families. It is a draughty corner, quite unlike Moray or even Banff, and runs down towards Aberdeen with the coast getting increasingly flat and uninteresting as it goes, turning into sand-dunes just north of the 'Granite City'. So different from the hinterland behind Banff, where the Deveron flows through splendidly pastoral country, lined with towers and castles, prosperous farms and hamlets, one spelt 'Kinneddar' and pronounced 'King Edward'! Scottish Nationalists make much of things like that but in this case miss the point. 'King Edward' is the name of a railway station, being built near one of that king's castles, not

A view of Craigston, near Banff, from the newly restored doocot. (Note the 'doos'.) The house was a seat of the Urquharts of Cromarty, of whom the best known was Sir Thomas Urquhart of that Ilk, translator of Rabelais.

actually at Kinneddar, and the romanticism of the railway authorities should be praised rather than damned. At Craignethan, for instance, in Lanarkshire, they did something similar, naming a station 'Tillietudlem', which was the fictitious name Scott gave the place.

Perhaps the best of the Deveron castles is Craigston, home of a cadet branch of the Urquharts of Cromarty, it having been built by 'the Tutor of Cromarty', that is, the uncle and guardian of the heir, in Jacobean times. He was the grandfather of the translator of Rabelais, a copy of which may be seen, with other works belonging to this most fantastical of Scotsmen, in the library on the top floor. Craigston escaped a face-lift while the Adam family were in the neighbourhood and has recently been renovated, doves put back in the long-empty dovecot. In design it was probably meant to emulate Fyvie, already across the Aberdeenshire border and often described as 'the glory of Scotch Baronial'. So it may be, but its plan and almost symmetrical main façades are not at all typical of Scottish style, even if the turrets and other details

are, being the creation of Alexander Seton, Lord Fyvie and later Earl of Dunfermline, Chancellor of Scotland and guardian of the royal infants, Elizabeth, future Queen of Bohemia, Henry, Prince of Wales, and Charles, who was to die the death of a martyr in 1649. The Chancellor made Fyvie symmetrical, large and grandiose after seeing things abroad and in the south, and he had the good sense not to pull down the older work but to repeat it in order to achieve the necessary symmetry. (This is precisely what Sir William Bruce did two generations later when he recast the Palace of Holyroodhouse for Charles II.) The Setons were the most important and influential Lowland family in the north-east until superseded to some extent by the Gordons, whose heiress married into them and founded a new family, the Seton-Gordons, ancestors of the celebrated Gordon Clan, including the earls and marquises of Huntly and Aberdeen and the poet Byron, whose mother was one. The Setons proper came to grief through their loyalty to the ill-fated House of Stuart. Yet Fyvie remains a memorial to that loyalty as it does to the superior taste and knowledge of its creator.

Fyvie stands on the site of another of King Edward's castles on the banks of the River Ythan, which flows east into the North Sea above Aberdeen. It is on the banks of the Ythan that Haddo House is built, another Adam mansion but altered during the last century when the Aberdeens were the friends of Gladstone and when Lady Aberdeen gave huge house-parties, the existing palatial interiors dating from then, as also the chapel and outbuildings which have proved such a boon to a later generation of lairds who interested themselves in music – the Haddo Music Festival won international renown. The house is now in the care of the National Trust for Scotland, which is not a bad fate after all that grandeur but presents a challenge to the Trust on how to maintain and display such palatial properties. It is one of the problems of inheriting such places that along with them goes the responsibility of keeping at least the appearance of a more spacious age and expansive social life, together with the furniture, pictures, silver and other treasures that belong. In England, I know that the experts of the Victoria and Albert Museum are sometimes called in to help with such matters; they display and care for the contents of Ham House, for instance. No doubt, as the Trust in Scotland acquires more and more properties of this kind, and as the task of looking after them becomes more exacting, the Royal Scottish Museum could play a similar role?

The Gordons were part Lowland, part Highland, their name being territorial, their ancestry both Norman and Border. They became the most powerful clan in the north-east, the Marquis of Huntly rejoicing under the title of 'Cock o' the North'. Huntly town is actually dull and grey, situated near the junction of the Deveron and the Bogie, Lowland and Highland rivers respectively. It does boast the well preserved and substantial remains of the erstwhile castle of the Seton-

Gordons – for one must really call them such even after changing their name. Huntly Castle is palatial; unlike most other local tower-houses, it rises not to a ring of picturesque turrets and crowsteps but to an elaborate fringe of Renaissance oriels and sculptured fenestration resembling Blois, where in the early-seventeenth century a Marquis of Huntly lived with his French spouse. It is a long rather than a tall building and is really a *château*.

Contending Forbeses claim that their manor-house at Druminnor was built first and that the 'palas' plan followed at Huntly was copied from their more ancient but modest seat. Druminnor is near Rhynie, where Highland and Lowland nomenclature merge, and has recently been restored after a partial demolition. It began life as a pele (a wooden palisade) erected around an artificial motte, or mount; then, in the fifteenth century, James II gave the laird permission to construct a stone tower and guard it with a yett – a strong iron gate. This has survived, though not the tower; that went in late Georgian times when baronialization occurred, only to be demolished recently. What is left is a long manor-house, almost barnlike in its simplicity, not unlike Huntly in embryo, with a round tower at one end and a series of vaulted lower storeys, a form very rare indeed for its date and place; it probably escaped destruction in its youth when the Forbes laird married into the Gordons. It stands on a small knowe on the edge of the Highlands as one runs down to the valley of the Don, which river waters Garioch, pronounced 'Gerry', former feudal fief of the sons and grandsons of the Normanizing Queen Margaret as earls of Huntingdon.

In Garioch and round-about, there has recently been a spate of buying-up and restoring, in some cases verging on rebuilding of castles and towers. The National Trust has acquired Craigievar, seat of the Forbes-Sempills, one of whom restored Druminnor in the 1960s. Midmar, perhaps the best preserved and least altered of all the so-called 'castles of Mar', has passed into new and richer hands for renovation. It was one of the places shown to the Queen Mother when she was

A view from the roof of Midmar Castle, Aberdeenshire, showing details of the turrets. This is one of the finest and least altered of all the 'Castles of Mar'.

castle-hunting in 1953 and might have made a good retreat, not too far from the rest of the family, had she not already more or less decided to save Barrogill. Crathes, also a Trust Property, is actually in Kincardineshire, which crosses the Dee around Banchory and takes in one of the most attractive slices of scenery in the area. Crathes was one of the earliest Jacobean castles to come to the Trust and was the home of an originally Saxon family, the Burnards, who became Normanized before travelling to Scotland with the feudal barons in the twelfth century and who, like the Irvines of Drum and their neighbours, have lived on Deeside ever since. Drum came to the Trust only a few years ago, its sturdy stone tower

Drum, near Banchory, seat of the Irvines since the fourteenth
and the battlemented medieval 'keep' erected on

This view shows the chapel (centre), the Carolean manor-house
 of Robert Bruce, to guard the Caledonian Forest.

Hay-making in the 'Gerry' near Chapel of Garioch.

pre-dating any others in the north and most others in Scotland, being built to guard the Caledonian Forest at the express behest of Robert the Bruce.

Then there is Fraser, another Trust Property, but only just, part harled and part not, and rather odd-looking in consequence. It stands in the middle of lowish green pastures and seems a trifle artificial, not only on account of its newish state but being so isolated, without defences; indeed, it is indefensible. It was built by one of the Bell family of masons responsible alike for Midmar and Crathes, and is Jacobean and Carolean, not feudal. Harthill is feudal, and its restoration, its transformation one might say, consequent upon the oil boom and the chance of a government grant, is probably the most spectacular of all such transformations in Aberdeenshire, or anywhere else. It rises close to a farm, beside a burn in the fields at the foot of Bennachie, that inimitable and impressive natural guardian of the 'Gerry' and eastern Aberdeenshire

The newly restored castle at Harthill with the slopes of Bennachie in the background.

generally. For centuries a ruin, Harthill has been completely reconstructed except for its ancient gatehouse, which, for some reason or another, has been left, tidied up, with a few flowers planted around and turned into a sort of folly, the rest being floodlit. Harthill is a real *coup de théâtre*, with high-level sentry's walk and gay, conically capped turrets, harled, but this was no doubt necessary with so much rebuilding in different materials. On the other hand, it can scarcely ever have looked in the past as it does now, though the restorers here have understood the real purpose of harling, which is not to make a contrast with the masonry but to complement it; thus at Harthill the same pinkish hues prevail throughout, so that one can with difficulty distinguish the naked stone from the harling. This is exactly as it should be, and it is as Craigievar and Crathes and Fraser were in the old days.

The towns and small burghs on the road down to Aberdeen are mostly in grey granite, bright and clean and prosperous-

*The inn on the Aberdeen Road at Old Meldrum, with a glimpse of the Hill
of Barra where Bruce defeated the Earl of Buchan in 1308.*

looking, each with its Presbyterian 'God-box' and slightly
more decorative 'Pisky' (Episcopalian) kirk, and each a Town
House with either tower attached or amusing bellcot. There is
a particularly fine one at Kintore dating from the seventeenth
century and approached by forestairs, and a rather excessively
ornate nineteenth-century one at Inverurie, which makes me
think of Spain and the richly flamboyant structures of Galicia.
This is another region where the very toughness of the
granite seems to provoke masons into even greater sculptural
efforts, into creating delicate lace-work pinnacles and other
features in a stone which, on the face of it, might better be
treated more ruggedly. The silhouette of the Marischal
College in Aberdeen is a case in point and recalls that of Milan
Cathedral rather than a Scottish seat of learning. Old
Meldrum boasts a small Continental-style 'place' as well as
the usual Town House and stands near Barra Hill, where Bruce
defeated the Earl of Buchan, and Norman power in the north

was broken – not that he, like Comyn, had not owed and paid suzerainty to Edward I as feudal lord, and with the other contenders to the Scottish throne was descended from a Norman grandmother. The distribution of the land then ensued, the Setons and Gordons getting a good share, so that Barra Castle was built by the former, and the district is actually now called after the latter.

It was a Seton too, Sir Alexander, who laid out the superb formal garden at Pitmedden, recently re-made by the National Trust for Scotland under the aegis of the late James Richardson, first Chief Inspector of Ancient Monuments for Scotland. Seton had studied law in Edinburgh and there saw the Renaissance gardens at Holyrood, currently being restored for the king, Charles II, by Sir William Bruce; happily for posterity, although those gardens have disappeared, the ones at Pitmedden have been reconstituted, using designs shown of them in a contemporary bird's-eye view made by the minister and laird of Rothiemay, the Reverend James

Where the river meets the sea – Brig o'Don, north Aberdeen.

A street in Old Aberdeen known as 'The Chanonry' on account of its being where the canons and clergy attached to the cathedral used to live.

Right: Douglas Simpson's Tower seen from the motte of the former Bishop's Castle, Aberdeen. Note the skyscrapers in the background.

Gordon. The scheme includes the use of coloured gravels to complement the box hedges and set patterns of flowers, as well as gay little garden pavilions in the French style.

The view westwards towards Bennachie is very fine, with its patchwork of fields and woods, so rich and fertile-looking that we forget for a moment where we are; and the spell is not seriously broken as one approaches Aberdeen. Oil has brought enormous prosperity and enormous changes, not all for the better, for affluence is a mixed blessing. Aberdeen has too much traffic and money. It is a city of glistening sky-scrapers, of wholesale demolitions and rebuildings, of wide

arteries leading in and out of the centre, of bustle and wealth putting one in mind more of rich Continental cities than of anything in Britain, least of all of a Scotland where the decaying older industrial districts have yet to find a new impetus or be done away with. In this sense, at least, the prosperity is exhilarating and not depressing; one seems to be going somewhere in a prosperous place, and although history has been put into the background with Aberdeen so busy making a 'bonny penny', there remain small corners of calm and antiquity, in Altoun and around the less ostentatious Don, less well known in its course than the Dee but deserving of attention. Symbol of this are the Brig o' Balgownie, said to have been built in the time of Robert the Bruce, the twin towers of St Machar's, the northernmost granite cathedral in Europe, and the late Douglas Simpson's tower, which he rescued from the middle of the town and had re-erected on the banks of the Don, opposite the grassy motte of the first episcopal castle. I had a letter about this from him the year before he died, confirming the origins and purpose of the motte.

One other part of Aberdeen that is not often seen by tourists, or by anyone else except fishermen and dockers, is the harbour, to which the granite towers and skyscrapers form an inimitable backcloth. On the far side is Torry, already in Kincardineshire but now a suburb of the city. Torry is the home of several entire communities of fishermen who came from the tiny villages down the coast when the fishing there became unprofitable; they arrived with their padres and all, they being Episcopalians as their counterparts in Buckie are mostly Roman Catholics or 'Closed Brethren'. Indeed, Kincardineshire was always a 'Pisky' and Jacobite stronghold, and in the old Tolbooth at Stonehaven the cell is shown where Episcopalian ministers were imprisoned for not praying for King George, thereby breaking the strict regulations regarding the propagation of their faith in the eight-

The spires and towerblocks of Aberdeen viewed from the busy harbour. It has a Hanseatic look.

The port of Stonehaven in Kincardineshire, filled with pleasure-craft. The fishing has largely moved north to Torry, a southern suburb of Aberdeen.

eenth century. It was not permitted for them to administer to more than five persons at a time, which rule led to some rather ingenious shifts, such as cutting holes between the floors of houses so that five persons could stand on each and hear the service from below. My father once toured the district on his bicycle and visited several such places.

Stonehaven has found a solution to the less lucrative state of the fishing and its latter-day concentration in Aberdeen and Torry by turning itself into a lively tourist-resort. Its harbour is full of pleasure-craft, small and large, their colourful sails and paintwork making the place gay and almost Mediterranean in good weather, when the North Sea is surprisingly blue. As a matter of fact, this part of the country has a much better climate, at least a drier one, than most of the rest of Scotland. No wonder the Prince Consort chose Deeside for the royal summer retreat, for it has weather not dissimilar in some ways from that of the Valais, in Switzerland, which can be almost Iberian at times. The coastal

Fiddes, a Kincardineshire farm in The Mearns near Laurencekirk.

climate here, despite the occasional haar, or sea mist, is more dependable in summer than further south, the main snag being the winter, when the road to Aberdeen can be iced up for long spells, the winds keeping it so. But Kincardineshire is not just a smaller version of Aberdeenshire, though it does take in part of Deeside and with it Banchory and one of the finest Scottish castles of the Jacobean period: it has its own character and accent. It also possesses a fertile inland region, The Mearns, which in reality is a continuation of Strathmore, or 'the Great Valley', running down behind the coastal hills and between them and the Highlands to Perth and the valley of the Tay.

Perhaps not quite so bonny as adjacent areas of Angus, but less rugged than Aberdeen, Kincardineshire was nevertheless occupied and developed by the feudalizing barons as long ago as the eleventh century, one such family, the Arbuthnotts,

A Sunday afternoon in summer in Glenbervie near Arbuthnott. The Bervie Burn waters The Mearns before flowing into the sea between Stonehaven and Montrose.

remaining *in situ* ever since. They came to Glenbervie in the wake of Queen Margaret and her sons and have served as secular and spiritual masters and mentors down the centuries – hence the remarkable little church at Arbuthnott, with its medieval tombs and tall Beauvais-style apse with priest's flat above. It was shared at one time by the Allardyce family, whose attractive manor-house has recently been renovated; but Arbuthnott House is the more interesting historically in that it shows in its various parts the whole history of its building and occupation since the Olifards and the de Swintons came here from Normandy via the Borders. They took the territorial name of Arbuthnott, also sometimes spelt with one 't', and the origin is Pictish, probably being spelt with a 'th' at the end before the advent of the Normans, who, as we know, could not pronounce such sounds. The Picts are particularly well remembered in Kincardineshire and Angus, in nomen-

The fortified kirk at Arbuthnott showing the fifteenth-century family aisle and the priest's 'flat' above (at right).

clature and in stone memorials, their sculptural talent surviving to this day. Arbuthnott House retains, encased within later walls, the shape of its ancient keep and possesses a Caroline addition with handsome plaster ceilings in the manner of those made at Holyrood for Charles II, when apprentice craftsmen 'did' many a country house for the better-off lairds, including the most northerly example of its kind at Brodie. To this was attached a Georgian façade, closing in the old courtyard and producing symmetry, the work of a Montrose mason whose bills still exist. The Arbuthnotts managed to have members on both sides during the Jacobite upheaval, thereby retaining their property and rights and acquiring as well five rather good Jacobite portraits of the 'King over the Water' and his family.

Kincardineshire ends just north of Montrose, in more genial climes, the rocky, indented coast giving place to lagoons and sandy beaches and, inland, the wide and verdant plain through which the North and South Esk rivers flow to the sea. At Dunnottar, however, a little south of Stonehaven, are the extensive ruins of the great castle of that name built on a headland jutting right out into the German Ocean and approached by a narrow, stony isthmus. Dunnottar was the seat of the Keiths, staunch Jacobites and Knights Marischal of Scotland. They were forced abroad during and after the Jacobite Rebellion and one became a general in the Russian Army and a field marshal in that of Frederick the Great; since then, Dunnottar has decayed in the salty winds to a rich iron shade not unlike the rock whence its buildings were hewn. It made history in the Cromwellian era when the governor's wife, Mrs Ogilvy, and the minister's wife from nearby Kineff hatched and carried out a daring plan to rescue 'the Honours of Scotland', the crown, sword of state and sceptre of the Stuart kings, which had been sent there for safety and which were in danger of capture by the Roundheads. The two ladies smuggled out the precious objects, bundling them up, and, with the connivance of the minister himself, they were hidden in a hole under the pulpit in Kineff Kirk. Dunnottar subsequently surrendered, but since the enemy was not Scots or Covenanting but English, the garrison was allowed to march out with drums beating and banners flying, and their lives were spared. Thus the episode was more honourable and heroic than many at this period, for Cromwell was not interested in revenge so much as in winning the war and occupying the country. A typical situation pertained at Airlie and Cortachy Castles, both Ogilvy seats, at about the same time. The Campbell Earl of Argyll attacked the first, Cromwell the second, with the result that Airlie was razed to the ground, the Earl himself assisting with an axe in its destruction, while Cortachy had its defences dismantled and was then handed back to its owners, Lady Ogilvy actually having returned to her certain objects looted by Cromwell's soldiery.

Highland Kincardineshire is best reached either from Stonehaven, along a beautiful undulating stretch of forest and moor, the hills reaching almost down to Lowland 'Stainie' itself and the sea, or via a quicker route from over Cairn o'Mount, on the west side of the Mearns. Here the road rises steeply and without warning straight into a land of heather and scrub, a grouse-moor which is often impassable in winter. At the meeting with the plain are a number of attractive villages. One, Fettercairn, boasts a triumphal archway at its southern entrance, commemorating the visit there in 1861 of Queen Victoria; she stayed at the local inn, 'The Ramsay Arms', incognito! A similar arch was erected at Edzell, over the border in Angus, but this time in honour of the Ramsay laird of the place, while a much more ornate version of both used to stand on the quayside at Dundee, facing Fife over the Firth of Tay. This was ruthlessly torn down to satisfy the delusions of grandeur of a modern generation when the Tay Road Bridge was built and the new road brought through traffic directly into the centre of the city.

The village of Fettercairn is relatively modern and replaces the old county town of Kincardine, whose castle at the foot of the pass over Cairn o'Mount was demolished in the seven-

teenth century, when Stonehaven became the 'capital'. The
mercat cross, however, is the original one. We are here
almost in Angus, and the Victorian archway might even
mark one's entry or departure, but before doing either one
must make a call at Balbegno. This belongs to the Gladstone
family, the same which reared the famous Prime Minister
whom Queen Victoria disliked so much, hence perhaps
Liberal influence hereabouts in the nineteenth century,
especially in the houses of the formerly staunchly Jacobite and
Tory gentry, along with the weekend parties and the church-
going, for Gladstone encouraged the lairds to support the
former Established Kirk, despite its Jacobite connections.
Balbegno is both Georgian and Jacobean, the latter portion
being a small castle attached to an equally modest eighteenth-
century country house, now a farm. In the older part there is a
most interesting Great Hall, its vaulted ceiling painted with
the armorial devices of the principal Scottish families and
done in the medieval style. The ecclesiastical-looking vaulting and 'medieval' heraldry used to fool visitors until it was
established that no part of the work pre-dates the reign of
James VI and I and that it represents, therefore, a very early
and rare form of Gothic-Revival!

Inverquharity, the restored 'keep' of the Ogilvys, with modern additions, beside the Carity Burn, Angus.

CHAPTER TWO

ANGUS AND FIFE

THOUGH ANGUS is very much a continuation of Kincardine-shire and itself continues little changed into Perthshire, in the great inland vale of Strathmore, there is a more obvious sense of well-being to be seen, perhaps partly induced by a redder, richer soil but also by the considerable increase in trees and the fact that it is further south. Angus is more sheltered from the winds, a bonny county, small but one in which some of the Scottish families most consistently loyal to the Stuarts have their seats, the Ogilvys at Cortachy and Airlie, the 'Bonnie Hoose o'Airlie' of the ballad, the Carnegies at Kinnaird, near Brechin, and the Bowes-Lyons at Glamis, not to mention the ruined redoubts of Cardinal Beaton at Melgund and the Lindsays at Edzell. The latter possesses the magnificent Jacobean garden created by Lord Lindsay in the early-seventeenth century and based directly on Continental models. As with the later one at Pitmedden, the Edzell 'pleasaunce', which includes bath- and summerhouses, has been recreated, this time by the Department of the Environment. Around a formal pattern of beds in which mottoes and insignia of the Lindsays appear is built a lovely red-sandstone wall, 'dished', or set back, in a chequerboard pattern to simulate the fess-chequey of the family coat of arms, with white and blue lobelia set against the red stone to make the correct heraldic colours, argent, azure and gules. Workmen came from Germany to open up neighbouring Glen Esk and start iron-mines there, and at least some of the features in the garden originated in them.

Ogilvy territory begins at Inverquharity, where the fifteenth-century stone keep erected by permission of James II of Scots has survived, replete with iron yett, all, in fact, but for a minor addition to the east which modern restorers have built up and incorporated in the same red sandstone as the original. Cortachy, nearby, is the present seat of the family, which since the last war has been able to demolish over thirty bedrooms, ballroom and other extensions erected in Gladstone's day when Countess Blanche, a Whig amongst Tories, went in for those political house-parties which were so important to Liberals in the nineteenth century and which almost ruined the Ogilvys. Happily, or so her successors would perhaps say, funds ran out before the Liberal Countess could enlarge and spoil Airlie, the more ancient Ogilvy seat, though she did have the park laid out in bridges and paths for a proposed visit by Queen Victoria which never materialized. Airlie was, as previously mentioned, virtually razed to the ground by a vengeful Earl of Argyll in the time of Charles I, and the lairds in the following century had to retreat to the Continent after the failure of two Jacobite risings in which they took a particularly active part, one founding an Ogilvy regiment abroad. He lived in France much of his life, and the story goes that, when in need of feminine company, he wrote to his wife in Scotland asking if he could take a mistress. She agreed, and no great harm seems to have been done in the process; and when at last Lord Airlie returned home, he was received as if nothing had happened. He then set about rebuilding Airlie Castle, of which little but a run of an outer wall and the entrance gateway stood. The present modest Georgian mansion, more like a large Angus farmhouse really, was the result, set behind the old battlements and providing the utmost privacy for three successive dowager ladies. Against an inner wall is planted the white Jacobite rose, taken from Achnacarry in Inverness-shire, whence came the bloom Prince Charlie wore, while in the big garden is a rare example

A rare sight in Scotland – a completely formal French parterre*, laid out at Airlie in the nineteenth century.*

in Scotland of the French *parterre*, the idea for which was brought back by the exiled laird, the '*bel Ecossais*' who, though he spoke Scots colloquially, did so with a strong French accent.

Perthshire begins on the south bank of the River Isla as it joins the Melgam burn below Airlie Castle, but slightly north is Kerry, or Kirriemuir, home of J. M. Barrie and always associated with *A House in Thrums*, though Kirriemuir gingerbread, with its picture of that house on the wrapper, is now made in East Kilbride, a 'new town' near Glasgow. Forfar is Kerry's larger rival, the county town of a county merged into the Region of Tayside, while Kincardineshire has been placed in Grampian. The names have some loose relevance, though not much more than those of Napoleon's *départements*, which were called after rivers and mountains and designed to break up the old provinces. To folk of my generation such efforts at the Napoleonization of Great Britain do not appeal and

hardly seem an improvement on what went before. In Fife
opposition was so firm that that 'kingdom', almost alone in
the country, managed to retain its identity in the new bound-
ary changes; Angus was demoted. Yet Forfar is not on
Tayside and is far from it in feeling. It was the town where the
Queen Mother was confirmed by the Bishop of Brechin and
will be associated in the minds of many with the jam and marmalade firm of Keiller's, from Dundee, whose cafés welcomed men stationed here during the war. Gone presumably
are the days when the weans, or small children, were given a
penny for handing in orange-peel they picked up, and when
girls were employed making wooden raspberry-pips for the
jam, as one told my father she did when he visited her in hospital; and gone, alas, is the original marmalade itself – almost,
for it is found more frequently nowadays in shops abroad
than at home.

Glamis, where the Queen Mother was not born but partly
brought up and where Princess Margaret was born, has been
fully described elsewhere, and often, yet it inevitably remains

*Left. Glamis, the rose-grey seat of
the earls of Strathmore and
Kinghorne and childhood home
of HM the Queen Mother.*

*The handsome crow-stepped
double doocot at Glamis which
has been nicely restored since
this photo was taken.*

the principal sight in Angus and draws both foreign tourists and local people. This is especially so since it became open more regularly a few years ago under the new Earl and Countess, who have made comfortable quarters and provided some privacy by converting the stables and yard into a house and entrance for themselves, giving over the historic parts of the castle to visitors. Glamis's picturesque, turreted outline must be almost the most famous and best known of its kind in the world, but its interior is less so and now much more interesting than heretofore. Lady Strathmore has found many things that lay in trunks or hung in cupboards and brought them out, including the little jester's costume worn by the Queen Mother's brother David at a fancy-dress ball when he went as her escort nearly seventy years ago, and which was actually the suit of the last private jester of any family in Scotland, the Bowes-Lyons retaining such a personage almost to within living memory. In trunks were found the costumes worn by many of the people whose portraits line the walls of the Great Hall, or upper drawing-room, and these have been cleaned and put on display, making a quite unique exhibition. Commensurate with all this revelation in the castle has been the tidying-up and displaying of the village of Glamis itself, notably of a row of typical Angus cottages in the Kirk Wynd which, in common with Barrie's birthplace at Kirriemuir, are in the care of the National Trust for Scotland; they also date from the seventeenth century, when Glamis Castle received its present romantic appearance, from a laird acting as his own architect and imagining he was making a mansion out of his ancestral fortalice, not the fairy fortress we think it today! Kirkwynd cottages have been turned into a folk museum, one of the best in the country, and these old houses, with the rest of Glamis, can now be explored in peace, since the village is bypassed by a new loop in the main road.

Kinnaird, the home of the Earl of Southesk, a Carnegie, is not open to the public and is so altered after three complete transformations, each made without destroying what went before but encasing it, that little of historic or architectural interest survives. The last architect engaged here was the arch-baronializer David Bryce, and Kinnaird has a near twin in the immense *château*-esque Fettes College in Edinburgh. Inside the castle, however, there is much of interest, for the lady of the house in early-Victorian times had been a friend of the Hamiltons, in Naples, and there are numerous Italian pictures on the walls and some amusing rustic touches in the grounds, her work. The Southesks were staunch Jacobites and only got their titles back about that time, which was lucky, since not long afterwards one of them married a royal princess. In the drawing-room are Kinnaird's greatest treasures, in the form of five authentic works by George Jamesone, 'the Scottish van Dyck' and limner to Charles I. They include contemporary Carnegies and the artist's acknowledged masterpiece, the young Montrose, then plain James Graeme. The future Covenanter-turned-royalist was seventeen years of age when this picture was painted and still a student at Aberdeen University but was enticed south to marry Lady Magdalen Car-

Lady Agnes's rustic summerhouse in the park at Kinnaird, near Brechin, Angus.

Brechin Cathedral, modern with a medieval bell-tower and 'Pictish' round tower, viewed from across the River Esk.

negie and to stay at Kinnaird until an heir had been born. This accomplished, he returned to his studies and subsequently did the Scottish version of the Grand Tour, studying languages, fencing and riding in Paris and Angers. His portrait hangs where it has always been, surrounded by those of his father- and uncles-in-law.

Kinnaird is between Brechin and Montrose, high above the River Esk as it winds towards the sea and its tidal lagoon. In the grounds is the charming little tower-house of Farnell, once the country residence, or *palatium nostrum*, of the bishops of Brechin. Edward I was here, and some small portion of the tower may date from his period, but most is fifteenth- and sixteenth-century, with interestingly decorated ecclesiastical ornament. Lord Southesk has had it restored, and Farnell is now let to friends. Brechin itself is a disappointing place: its site is fine, beside the river, but its former cathedral has been rebuilt at least as often as Kinnaird Castle and without leaving the shell of what went before, its main attraction lying in two towers, one medieval, the other 'Pictish', both of which rise in a tolerable state of authenticity beside a rather uncomplementary barn-kirk. The Picts, as earlier mentioned, had their stronghold hereabouts, and between Forfar and Brechin may be seen some remarkable Pictish stones, just by the roadside at Aberlemno, and others in Aberlemno kirk. Brechin also boasts a castle, a handsome Palladian mansion designed by a clergyman friend of Sir William Bruce, who copied that master's approach by filling in the space between two old round towers and letting a bit of the ancient castle survive behind his elegant new façades. Generally, however, the town suffers as some others in the country do from local vandalism; the notices put up announcing Brechin as a 'cathedral city', and also one commemorating the erection of some rather good new council houses, were defaced and torn down almost as soon as they went up. I spent a Sunday morning there not so long ago, taking pictures for my *Scotland's Abbeys and Cathedrals*, and was quite appalled by some of the minor destruction and thoughtlessness I saw, also by the bad taste and vulgarity of some of the shops and modernized properties. It seemed pretty clear that informed preservation had not yet arrived here, though Brechin is nothing to Montrose, where official vandalism over the past twenty years has been notorious.

The fate of old Montrose was exposed in detail by the late Duncan Fraser, who, seeing no other way of saying what he had to say and which needed saying, published his own books in his own printing-works in the town, the Standard Press. In one particularly telling reference he showed two photographs of the High Street, in the second of which only two buildings appearing in the first remained as built. The gaudy shopfronts would not disgrace some southern English High Street, but they do disgrace that of a decent Angus burgh; they also insult the nineteenth-century statuary of local worthies. The few trees and other attractive features that survive now only hinder through-traffic that is forced to wind its way in and out of the place in competition with local shoppers and parkers. Montrose is prosperous, growing ever more so as a result of the oil for which it is a supply-base, and it is perhaps ironic that some of the port's best surviving buildings line part of the old harbour in a dignified and ample manner.

It would be stretching things a bit to describe Montrose as yet another 'Venice of the North', but its site is worth some association of that kind, having a harbour opening directly to the North Sea, though protected, and a vast inner basin which provides a marvellous place for small boats and fishermen. The coast southwards is not so rocky and indented as in its Kincardine equivalent, but with wide sandy bays ending in fine headlands, such as Lunan, with Red Castle at one end, a paradise for children and parents, so long as one does not go there at a weekend. Between it and Arbroath, with its own fine beach, cliffs and caves to boot, is Auchmithie, famous for 'smokies' – not kippers but haddock.

Arbroath itself rejoices, like Stonehaven, in two roles, that of port and resort. Its red stone is really red, quite inimitable, and helps to create a remarkable unity in the architecture of the place, except for the handsome white lighthouse on the front which seems intended as part of 'the fun of the fair'. My sister was born in Arbroath, and I was supposed to have been – I certainly disported myself in my birthday suit on the beach there, as a family photo proves, but I did not actually arrive there. In any case, my love of history, even as a small child, was so strong that no beach nor anything else can surpass it, and Arbroath to me, therefore, is Arbroath Abbey and the exploits of its abbot, who, surely though, did not put a bell on Inchcape in order to lure ships onto it nor use the great rose window of his abbey kirk as a lantern to misguide mariners? The abbot's lamp must have been meant to guide ships safely into the harbour of Aberbrothock. Robert Stevenson, grandfather of Robert Louis, when he came to design the Bell Rock Lighthouse on that tiny islet, which is covered by sea except for an hour or two each day, said after visiting the site in a rowing-boat that there was no evidence that anyone had ever placed a bell there at any time, not even 'Ralph the Rover', as Southey's poem avers.

The Pends, once part of the abbey at Arbroath. The famous reply to the Pope, Scotland's Magna Carta, was signed in a room above.

Round the corner from Arbroath as one approaches the mouth of the Tay, the landscape becomes warm and wooded as if one were already inland. It is the eastern end of what to the west of Dundee is called 'The Carse of Gowrie', a region well known for fruit-growing, especially raspberries, all facing south, with high protective hills behind and the sea in front to keep the frosts away. The coastal resorts on the Firth of Tay succeed each other almost into Dundee; they look across to north Fife and a sea and landscape that in imagination leads ever southwards, to Edinburgh and the Border. I sometimes wonder if Dundonians often view their city from the Fife side and, if they do, what they think of it. On a fine day the scene is not too bad: the background of the Sidlaws, the two bridges, railway and road, and a few, very few decent buildings. If one knows where to look, there is Dudhope Castle, for which no use seems yet to have been found; it was

A view of the Tay and the Perthshire hills from the Fife shore, with New-burgh on the left.

the seat of Claverhouse, the 'Bonnie Dundee' of the ballad. It is easy to make out the singular tower of the Town Kirk and the steeple of Sir George Gilbert Scott's cathedral, but that is about all; the rest is skyscrapers rising in tiers from the remaining indigenous rows, to make one think more of North America than anywhere else, not Scotland; on a dull day the view is positively repellent. Dundee's environs, on the other hand, as with many Scottish cities, are fine, not only along the coast but through the hills into Strathmore and on into the Highlands, and more especially across the Tay into Fife. St Andrew's University has been merged with that in Dundee, the more gentle researches still being made in the former as befits its antiquity and erstwhile ecclesiastical status, with the ruder, more modern faculties housed in Dundee. Indeed, north Fife and southern Angus are very close in many ways, scenically as well as culturally, and

Dundee and the Tay Railway Bridge viewed from Peashills, North Fife.

would have been joined in a single region but for Fife's successful battle to retain its identity entire.

Some Dundonians commute northwards into Perthshire, but the most salubrious suburbs are on the Fife side of the Firth of Tay, this being encouraged during the last century by the coming of the railway and the completion of the notorious bridge, which had to be rebuilt and realigned after its fatal collapse. Commuting between Wormit and the city was always a matter of minutes, as for Tayport and Newport-on-Tay. The denizens of these airts must have watched the skyline opposite degenerate into the standardized one of high-rise blocks, but they can always look eastwards out to sea or westwards to the mountains of Perthshire for relief and, indeed, enjoy one of the most expansive and delightful panoramas in Scotland.

The climate across the bridges has always been noted for its

mildness, so that at Balmerino and Lindores the monks built
two of their most celebrated abbeys. Lindores, in the west,
was where fruit-culture was first introduced into the district,
and amongst the enigmatic ruins of that once large and flourishing abbey the remains of old trees can still be seen. At
both Balmerino and Lindores the monks made water-mills as
well, and two of these survive, one at each end, while at Balmerino the earliest-recorded Spanish chestnut to be planted in
Scotland was introduced by the Cistercians. It survives, held
together with chains, gnarled and bent.

Fife is known as 'the kingdom' on account of its having
formed one of seven Pictish sub-kingdoms, the name 'Pit',
which is frequent, denoting the presence of these now extinct
people – extinct in the sense that their name and power have
gone, but surely a whole race, the original natives of most of
Scotland, cannot have become extinct like the Dodo? They
were engulfed by the Scots coming from Ireland in much the
same way as the red squirrel has been engulfed by the grey in
some quarters, but not wiped out. Pitscottie, Pitlessie and
Pittenweem are just three of the Pictish names of Fife; there
are very many more, some relating merely to farms and
homesteads dotted about the 'kingdom'. St Andrews, of
course, has little to show in this context, for it is medieval and
Renaissance, having passed out of significant history, or
nearly so, at the time of the Reformation, when its priory-
cathedral was evacuated and despoiled; parts of the present
burgh were built out of looted masonry.

There was a slight revival of fortunes in the mid-
seventeenth century when, in lieu of the old cathedral, Holy
Trinity became the seat of Protestant archbishops, one of
whom, John Spottiswood, crowned Charles I and tried to
revive an interest in decent ecclesiastical architecture in Scotland, building the amusing little Gothic-Revival kirk at
Dairsie alongside his country residence. James Sharp, or
Shairp, earned the eternal hatred of the Covenanters by
accepting the primacy under Charles II and was murdered for
his pains on Magus Muir, just outside St Andrews, in front of

The Archbishop's Castle, St Andrews. After the murder of Cardinal Beaton, John Knox and those concerned were imprisoned here before being sent to the galleys.

his kneeling, pleading daughter. There are monuments both to his murderers and to him on the site, and also a grandiose one in black-and-white marble in Holy Trinity, where the funeral oration was given with the dead Archbishop's blood-soiled rochet draped over the pulpit. In his *Cevennes Journal*, Robert Louis Stevenson, describing the Pont de Montvert, writes about the Camisards, or Languedoc Protestants, mentioning how it was there that "these southern Covenanters slew their Archbishop Sharp". He goes on to speak of the persecution on the one hand, the febrile enthusiasm on the other, and how "it is almost equally difficult to understand in these quiet, modern days, and with our easy modern beliefs and unbeliefs". *Tout ça change*, we might add. In St Andrews, golf has largely taken the place of former fervour and bigotry in much the same way as cricket has in English towns.

St Andrews does have a kind of Englishness, a suggestion of Oxford in its stone buildings and general character, with two parallel streets, North and South, roughly corresponding to the Broad and the High, and students riding about on bicycles with baskets on the handlebars. They often wear red togas, or gowns, which makes a Sunday-morning promenade along the pier colourful and gay in this otherwise grey little town by the sea. (The 'bejants', or 'freshers', also have university 'mothers', though few of them need looking after these days.)

St Andrews is not, however, the county capital; that is Cupar, or rather used to be until the 'new town' of Glenrothes usurped that position. Fife has always had two faces, perhaps three, but two which the first king of Great Britain referred to in his description of the 'kingdom' as "a beggar's mantle fringed with gold". In those days coal and salt were exported to the Continent, making the coastal fringe rich, and as yet the Howe, or central plain, had not been developed as it was to be during the Agricultural Revolution and was therefore poor by comparison.

Cupar is the seat of the North-East Fife District Council; it is not an old-looking town, very much of the eighteenth and nineteenth centuries, but prosperous and a typical farming centre. There is still an artificial motte, or mound, to recall antiquity and former importance, though nothing like, say, Falkland, where the bulk of the Stewart palace survives. Here James V, father of Mary, Queen of Scots, died on hearing of her birth, fearing it would mean the end of the dynasty. The ill-fated Queen loved to go to Falkland for the hunting, and it was there that Charles II first constituted the Scots Guards from troops specially chosen to guard him. Round about, the small Royal Burgh is full of interesting old houses, many once the homes of courtiers at the miniscule but beautiful palace; one is still thatched, which many in central Fife once were but are now pantiled, the tiles coming back as ballast from Belgium in Jacobean times. The whole of Falkland is now a Conservation Area, with the National Trust for

Rural humour outside a farm near Ceres, central Fife. The cock was once a weather-vane on a kirk tower.

Scotland Heritable Deputy Keepers of the Palace and with a Hereditary Constable, Captain and Keeper for Her Majesty the Queen. The gardens have been re-created according to the plan of James V, and an attempt has been made to revive the atmosphere of the sixteenth century in the interior. There is also a well preserved 'real tennis' court, the only other original one extant in Britain being at Hampton Court; both are still used.

Most people who know central Fife would agree that Ceres, or St Cyr, is the most typical and best-maintained village in a county, and indeed a country, where proper villages are rather rare. By this I mean that Scottish villages did not grow, as English ones did, around a manor-house and church but more likely round a farm, which grew to hamlet proportions, with a kirk, a school and possibly an inn, all scattered about, often a mile or so apart. Such an arrangement

The fine eighteenth-century town steeple at Auchter-muchty, central Fife, typical of the region.

Right: The octagonal Georgian doocot at Wester Pitkierie, East Neuk o'Fife. Note the pigeons foraging.

exists at Dunino, on the road from Anstruther to St Andrews, which announces itself some 2 miles from its extremely modest 'centre', the latter consisting of a school and sub-post office, and a few rural houses; the church is somewhere else, also the local 'big house', and there are several farms in this community which covers an area some 4 miles across. Ceres, on the other hand is a recognizable village, built near a great house and an ancient church, with two inns and a village green on which games are performed in summer. Then there are the numerous Royal Burghs in Fife, usually made so because their inhabitants performed some service to the king at Falkland. Auchtermuchty, for example, was where the

gleds, or falcons, were kept for the hunt, and at Strathmiglo the bread was baked. These and some other places have handsome town steeples reminiscent of Belgian belfries and mostly of good Renaissance pattern of low-pointed steeple and balustraded gallery, with prison or tolbooth and council chamber below, approached via forestairs. Auchtermuchty was also noted for its thatch, the reeds coming from Lindores Loch or the banks of the Tay, but today there are no more thatchers, and the one house I know to have been re-thatched recently was done by a man from Norfolk.

The East Neuk o'Fife, or easternmost corner, almost all on the sea, is the favoured place for tourists and also for fishing – and for retired professors and lecturers from St Andrews, they mostly preferring Crail, while the holiday-makers have their camp at Anstruther, and fishing-headquarters are at Pittenweem. Elie no longer fishes but is a haven for folk from Edinburgh and the south.

Slightly inland are Balcaskie and Kellie, the former the first home of the first professional Scottish architect, Sir William

The front of Earlshall, Fife, restored by Sir Robert Lorimer at the end of the nineteenth century.

Bruce, who also helped Charles II to return from Holland. Kellie is a superb specimen of a Scots baronial residence that grew down the centuries to become several houses of different periods yet homogeneous in spite of it. It was the seat in Norman times of a Saxon family, then of the Oliphants and the earls of Kellie. Until it became National Trust property, with Hew Lorimer as guardian, it was the home of the Lorimers – of Professor Lorimer who repaired it so sympathetically, of his son John, who also restored and lived in an old sea-captain's house down by the harbour at Pittenweem, and then of Hew and his family. Sir Robert, the famous architect, was brought up there and laid out the garden, a clever amalgam of old Scotch forms and current ideas, not wholly uninfluenced by the work of Gertrude Jekyll, though one must be careful and not say that too loudly in Lorimer company. Sir Robert may, perhaps, have arrived at much the same conclusions as she and Sir Edwin Lutyens did at the same time, as the French insist they did *vis-à-vis* the Italians and the Renaissance. At any rate, the result is entirely satisfactory and Scottish. At Earlshall, Lorimer's first restoration and garden-creation *in toto*, one can see his ideas more fully developed, for herbaceous borders, so popular in the south, do find a place, together with formal topiary, a herb-garden and park, the latter directly visible from the windows of the main rooms, not away in the distance.

The coastal burgh I know best is Pittenweem, where I spend three nights of every week in The Priory, which is the oldest parsonage and longest continuously occupied ecclesiastical building in Scotland. The lower floors are vaulted and date from the fifteenth and sixteenth centuries, with late-Stuart rooms over and Georgian ones above them. In the garden is the prior's entrance to St Fillan's Cave and Holy

A view from the Priory at Pittenweem, with the entrance to St Fillan's Cave right and houses round the old harbour beyond.

*The medieval gatehouse to St Adrian's Priory, Pittenweem, the oldest con-
tinuously inhabited ecclesiastical foundation in Scotland.*

Well, which was used as such before the tenth century,
though the priory itself was not founded until the twelfth,
when the monks came over to the mainland from the Isle of
May. The building overlooks the entire burgh, notably the
harbour which the monks created and first used and that
rather special group of tall, pantiled and crow-stepped houses
round the quayside. It was down there, at what is called 'The
Gyles' (the name probably deriving from a Dutch word
describing a process of brewing) that John Lorimer, painter
and elder brother of the architect, had his second house –
indeed two houses, one, separated from the other by a few
yards, where he put his guests. The National Trust for Scotland rebuilt the group between, including one that was formerly the town house of the Anstruthers, who came to Fife in
the eleventh century from southern Italy and have been in the

Boat-building at Easter Anstruther harbourhead, a rare sight these days.

county ever since. They kept their fox-hounds in a barnlike building behind, which became a chapel before being restored as a house. Taken together, Trust and private property around the old harbour at Pittenweem make one of the most attractive scenes in eastern Scotland and appear regularly on picture-postcards and calendars.

If Pittenweem is the hub of the fishing-industry in the East Neuk, Anstruther thrives on a combination of tourism and boat-building, its huge harbour almost empty because the fish-market is not there and the dues are thought to be high. Boat-building also goes on at neighbouring St Monans, which is a quaint little place with a great deal of unspoilt character. There have been restorations there as well, but more intriguing to me at least are some of the local names which have a foreign ring about them – Montador, for

Left: Looking through the garden gate of Kilrenny Manse, the oldest in Scotland, though built as a private residence. Right: 'Caribbean Princess', a figurehead in a garden at Pittenweem, recalling the time when East Fifers sailed the Seven Seas and when the fishing-industry had not yet been established here.

instance, which is surely Spanish? The Armada did, in fact, come this way, and at Anstruther the captain of a Spanish galley asked for shelter for himself and his sailors. The parish minister, understanding Latin, was able to converse with him, and afterwards some of the men stayed behind. The manse, where part of the parley took place, is still lived in by the local minister. Other influences are of a different nature: Mrs Bennet, sister of the late Dr James Richardson of Ancient Monuments, told me once how in conversation with a dusky-looking lady in Pittenweem she was told, "Most of us have some coloured blood in us." "Not me," replied Mrs Bennet; but it is true in many cases, possibly following men going to the whaling and further afield in the days of the sailing-boats, before coastal fishing took over. Mrs Bennet had in her garden a figurehead called 'Caribbean Princess', and in the kirkyard at Anstruther there is a monument to a Tahitian chieftainess and her husband; she lived in a large nineteenth-century house nearby still known as 'The Palace'.

Westwards from Elie and Earlsferry, whence a ferry ran between the 'kingdom' and the Lothians in the old days, landscape and occupations change. There is very little fishing, and it is getting less with the increasing pollution of the Firth of Forth from excess domestic and industrial sewage. I have seen the water bright red at Granton on occasion, near an inkfactory. Leven is industrial, and so is Kirkcaldy, which since the decline of coal-mining and ancillary work has taken over from Dunfermline as the principal town in west and southern Fife. Kirkcaldy is go-ahead and lucky in its advisers, architectural and otherwise, so that progress has not spoiled the town as much as might have been the case. There has been a certain

Sundown over the Firth of Forth – a view from Elie, with castellated lighthouse. The Earlsferry used to ply from near here to and from North Berwick.

The mill at Lathallan, near Colinsburgh, has recently been restored and not only makes its own electricity but grinds meal. Note the mill-lade and drying-kiln hopper.

Right: The interior of the meal-mill at Lathallan showing the seventeenth-century grinding-stone still functioning.

amount of demolition which could have been avoided, and some nice rows of vernacular houses have been replaced by tall concrete blocks, but it has not been haphazard, and now that it is over, the result must appear not too bad to those who did not know Kirkcaldy well beforehand.

Dunfermline has not been so lucky. It was the capital of Scotland in late-Pictish and early-Norman times, the seat of Malcolm Canmore and his Saxon spouse, the saintly Queen Margaret. They founded its abbey and palace, bringing to this ancient Celtic seat the learning and experience of Durham and Canterbury. In the now-ruined palace, Elizabeth, 'The Winter Queen', ancestor of our own Queen, was born, also

the future Charles I. Since then Dunfermline has found greater glory in the memory and gifts of Andrew Carnegie, who almost put it on the map again. Since the war, however, the slow decline has continued, and the only solution so far seems to have been to make a wide, easy-to-drive bypass where motorists who should be doing 30 miles per hour are encouraged to do more. Curiously enough, the Dunfermline police have a habit of setting up radar-traps on the outskirts of small neighbouring villages, especially at holiday weekends, where most of the catch are Sunday motorists who normally drive around the prescribed speed or a few miles above, their licences are endorsed, and they are fined, but to what end? The habitual breakers of the Highway Code, the road-hogs and aggressive lorry- and van-drivers, are not about on such occasions. The various summonses resulting from these holiday excesses emanate from the Sheriff Court, the old building of which is perhaps the only really important one in Dunfermline other than the abbey and ruined palace of the Scottish kings. It has an elegant steeple with colonnades and the beginning of an arched 'piazza', and some years ago it was proposed to remove it and erect a large steel-and-concrete 'complex' in the style of other contemporary all-purpose centres. As representative of the Scottish Georgian Society, I was one of those involved in trying to save Dunfermline from making such a blunder, and happily we were successful.

Probably the future of Dunfermline lies more and more in its proximity to and association with Edinburgh. Once the new Forth Road Bridge was opened, this seemed a foregone conclusion. In clear weather I can see the place, even the steeple of its Georgian Sheriff Court, from my windows high up in the New Town of Edinburgh, and now that one does not have to go by ferry, it is almost a dormitory adjunct of the capital. Robert Bruce's bones were said to have been discovered in the nineteenth century when a perfectly hideous mock-Gothic choir was added to the beautiful Durham-style nave of the abbey-kirk, presently in the care of Ancient Monuments. Unfortunately the discovery has never properly been authenticated, but it was commemorated on the top of the new central tower with balustrading composed of the words "KING: ROBERT: THE: BRUCE", which four-sided banality could scarcely be bettered. This sort of thing certainly indicts the perpetrators, and their successors, for it was the same 'Battle-of-the-Styles' architect employed here who ruined the external appearance of St Giles High Kirk in Edinburgh – all, that is, except for its historic crown-steeple.

Between Dunfermline and its rival Kirkcaldy, birthplace, by the way, of Robert Adam and Adam Smith, lies Burntisland, which is not an island but a decaying port partly brought back to life by the aluminium-industry, the deposit of waste bauxite rendering whole hillsides red and unproductive, even poisoned. Nearby, however, there is a charming little 'riviera' centring on Aberdour and Inchcolm, which is an island, 'the Iona of the East', where Celtic Christianity and afterwards Roman flourished till the Reformation and left the most complete domestic group of monastery buildings in Scotland, saved from the same destruction as the church by being turned into a private house for the Earl of Moray. At Inverkeithing some belated efforts have been made to rescue the remnants of 'Queen Annabella's Palace', really a Fran-

A derelict boarding-house by the harbour at Burntisland, with the recently restored castle behind. It does not snow very often along this coast.

ciscan convent in which the royal lady stayed, and a bit of an older quarter where there are grouped a parish kirk, with a fine tower and medieval font, a handsome eighteenth-century Town House and one of the best-preserved medieval mercat crosses in the country. It is replete with its original heraldry, ecclesiastical, royal and civic, and has recently been tinctured up most beautifully. In fact, the cross was moved from its old position for safety and placed in an attractive cul-de-sac with ancient buildings in the vicinity.

From here, Edinburgh and the two bridges over the Forth dominate the view, as they do on the Dunfermline side, from Rosyth, where the Navy are in command. Beyond, as far as the Kincardine Bridge, are coal-mines, some very modern with tunnels connecting them up, full mechanization and underground transport systems. This is particularly interesting and appropriate since it was here, at Culross, that Sir

George Bruce, knighted by James VI and I when he visited the place, installed a simple but effective underground drainage-system so that the mines could be worked under the Firth of Forth. He installed a continuous bucket-arrangement to keep the tunnels dry, taking his sovereign below and bringing him up on an island in the middle of the Firth of Forth at low tide. That jittery monarch immediately took fright, fearing yet another attempt on his life, and it was probably as much through a sense of relief as anything else that his host was honoured when they both returned to dry land. Culross was once in Perthshire, being at the western end of Fife, almost as far away from St Andrews and the East Neuk as Edinburgh is from Berwick. It was founded by monks – indeed, St Mungo, or Kentigern, was said to have been educated here by St Serf. Certainly there was a Cistercian abbey there, part of which stands in the present manse garden; another part is incorporated within the parish kirk, and more remains lie in the grounds and under Culross Abbey House. This was built by Sir William Bruce's uncle and was probably the first Scottish house of its size to show genuine Renaissance influence, its builder having been at Court in the south and become familiar with the great houses of England.

Culross is now a showpiece, a showpiece of Jacobean Scotland as it was in the years just before the Union of the Crowns in 1603, and shortly afterwards. It decayed and became a gracious reminder of another age and of past prosperity, an age when Scottish domestic architecture reached the height of its own particular form and remained static. So it came down to us, a little grubby and a backwater but now all spruced up by the National Trust and the Department of the Environment as a model for others. Sir George Bruce's little 'palas' (the name indicates a long rather than a tall building, a 'place' as opposed to a tower) was obviously meant to imitate a burgher's house in Bruges or Antwerp, whence he sent his exports. It wore its age well, even its professional restoration by experts of the Ancient Monuments Department, until a recent covering of masonic 'porridge' was slopped over every-

A cobbled street in Culross, west Fife, with Bishop Leighton's Lodgings, since harled, on the left.

thing, crowsteps, chimney-copes, door- and window-jambs, the lot, when all its charm and historic interest evaporated. Then there is the Netherlandish-looking Town House, more elegant and a century later, so far allowed to speak for itself and not over-restored; plus a whole street, or causeway, of genuine cobbles, not smooth, regular setts but rough stones of differing sizes, good for getting the water away. A specimen section of this has been repaired and 'done up' for posterity, around a score or more houses, including 'The Study', a tall, miniature Scots baronial pile, a town house with turret and spiral stair and shutter-board windows – that is, with fixed top glazing and open at the bottom except for wooden shutters. Not far off is Bishop Leighton's Lodging, recently harled and whitened though not needing it. He was Bishop of

Dunblane and later Archbishop of Glasgow in the reign of Charles II, and saintly successor to the ill-fated James Sharp. He tried very hard to reconcile Presbyterians and Episcopalians but, failing to do so, retired to the south of England, where he died broken-hearted.

Culross is no longer a port, for the tidal Forth has shifted its shore, and it has a Lowry-like view, minus the people, looking over the water towards a weird, other-worldly panorama of petrol-refineries and factories such as would not disgrace that of Mestre seen from Venice. When the wind blows in the wrong direction, the smell is commensurate with the ugliness of the aspect, yet Culross was not in the past the clean, bright place it is now; it could never have been, either when the mines functioned nor with the salt-panning. This was a process whereby sea salt was evaporated in large, low, iron pans, which were heated underneath by smouldering secondary coals. The smoke, stour and smell must have been quite as bad as that which emanates from Grangemouth and the environs of Falkirk today, and much nearer to the sufferers, though there were well planted gardens in ancient Culross, the monks saw to that, and it was celebrated for its orchards, the climate being excellent and entirely different from its hinterland, inland and higher up. Much of west Fife consists of windswept hills, with few trees and not particularly gay villages composed largely of council houses, Scotland having more per head than any other part of Britain, or indeed Western Europe.

This bleak upland airt is in complete contrast not only to anything along the coast but to most of the rest of inland Fife, around Falkland or Cupar; it is not genial, and it is little known and looks towards the first foothills of the Highlands, the Ochils and the upper Forth valley around Stirling. It was part of Perthshire originally, with Culross, but, unlike tiny Kinross-shire, which it almost surrounds, it was not handed over to the new Tayside Region but left intact, part of Fife, in the recent boundary-changes.

The last place in the 'kingdom' is Kincardine, where the first of the modern bridges to cross the Forth east of Stirling was built. The burgh is a sorry place now but mercifully half bypassed by the new road, which literally looks down on it. It is full of decaying mills and once-charming old houses, definitely a burgh whose glory has faded, for it must have been important in Jacobean times, like Culross; the ferry ran here, and there was a market, the local laird securing that right for Kincardine in the early-seventeenth century, as witness the Cross with his arms upon it surviving. Today there is the view towards Grangemouth and Falkirk, slightly more slanted than from Culross, a huge power-station on either side, enormous pylons marching over water and fields all round; behind, believe it or not, are three high-rise blocks, modern versions of village architecture in industrial Scotland.

The Carse, or plain, in the Forth Valley below Stirling, viewed from Clackmannan Tower.

CHAPTER THREE

KINROSS, PERTH AND STIRLING

TO THE IMMEDIATE west of Kincardine lies Clackmannanshire, with a few hills to break the monotony of the flatness of
the district, unusual for Scotland and almost Dutch in
feeling. Commensurate with this too are the long, low lines
of cottages, still mostly inhabited despite the propinquity
of the aforementioned skyscrapers, power-stations and
generally large and unmannerly neighbours. They are single-
storeyed and are finished at the eaves with shell-shaped skew
putts, curly-whirly stones at the eaves where the gables end.
Clackmannanshire has been lumped with the Central Region
and Stirling, and sizable slices of both Highland and Lowland
Perthshire, but it was once Scotland's smallest county and in
common with Kinross used to share a sheriff and other of-
ficials within the 'kingdom' of Fife. It is actually on Forth-
side and contiguous with West Fife, but "What's in a name?"
It boasts a minute capital which is not unattractive and which
is proud of its 'Clack', a prehistoric boulder that stands beside
a handsome mercat cross and Town House in the square. The
town steeple, incidentally, is of the same period and design as
the one at Culross and is capped with a similar ogee-roofed
cupola.

On a hill overlooking the Forth, no longer a firth but now a
river, is Clackmannan Tower, which belonged to the Bruces,
of the same family as the worthy knight who brought prosperity to Culross in Jacobean times and Sir William Bruce,
Architect Royal to Charles II, but earlier, through an illegit-

imate descent from the royal House. It remained inhabited until the end of the eighteenth century when the widow of the last of that particular line occasionally amused herself by knighting chosen friends and relations with Robert Bruce's two-handed sword, or claymore – or so it was reported. She would have found this quite a job, for the size of the weapon and its weight, it being normally borne on the back, or carried by a sword-bearer and wielded as a *coup de grâce.* Bruce's sword belongs to the present Earl of Elgin and Kincardine, who is of that Ilk and lives between Dunfermline and Culross, his mother staying at Culross Abbey House – which shows how strong and lasting are the historical and family traditions in Lowland Scotland, at least as strong as those of the Highlands and usually better authenticated, despite revolutions, religious and secular, and the shifting of boundaries.

At Menstrie, on the road to Stirling and still in Clackmannanshire, is the 'utterly' restored castle, really the old manor-house of Viscount Canada, under which grandiose and evocative title Sir William Alexander was known after the founding of Nova Scotia in the early-seventeenth century. His ancestors were called MacAlister and came here with another Highlander, the first Campbell to try his hand as courtier to the king at Stirling in the days before Flodden. Menstrie was one of the earliest test-cases when the local authority wished to demolish it and build a housing-estate on the site. The National Trust for Scotland and other bodies protested, and in due course a compromise was arrived at whereby the 'castle' was restored and made the central feature in a group of council houses. One is bound to doubt the efficacy of this solution, especially when any suggestion of antiquity or historic atmosphere has been almost wholly lost in the exercise. Menstrie looks completely out of place where it is and as it is, though there is an interesting room inside, decorated with the shields of the baronets of Nova Scotia, themselves surrounding a portrait of Charles I, in whose reign the first creations were made and to whom Sir William Alexander was devoted.

Castle Campbell in its eyrie-like setting in the Ochils above Dollar, Clackmannanshire.

Recently I heard that an acquaintance was not available because he was "holidaying in Clackmannanshire". I could not for the life of me think exactly where that could be until I remembered Dollar, a delightful little spa in the lea of the Ochils, just where Perthshire and Kinross-shire meet this tiny county. The nomenclature is curious, for 'Dollar' is sometimes spelt 'Dolour', and the Burn of Sorrow runs down from 'Castle Gloume' between the houses and under the main street. The castle is now named after the Campbells, who made it their Lowland redoubt in the years preceding the Reformation, when John Knox is said to have stayed there. With Dollar itself, Castle Campbell is definitely worth a visit; the small town is very pleasant, popular as a long-distance weekend resort for discriminating Glaswegians, warm and nicely wooded, with a fine neo-classical academy and a good view towards the Forth and in the direction of Stirling. The

"The most regular piece of architecture in the kingdom": Kinross House, viewed from the avenue.

Glen of Sorrow reminds me of New Zealand, so natural and unspoilt is it, and the castle should be approached on foot, up the glen, not by car unless one is absolutely pressed for time. It sees everything yet is unseen itself, and is partly inhabited; but it is the site that matters, the winding path through the trees and across bridges to it and the background of barish hills, grazed by sheep, smooth except for the occasional rowan or bracken gracing the edge of some brown, tumbling burn.

Eastwards from Dollar is Kinross-shire, a very wet county. This is because, lying on high land in the middle of what might be called the Fife peninsula, it catches everything coming up from the west. In compensation, however, Kinross is scenically attractive and was the home of three of Scotland's and one of Europe's foremost architects, Sir William Bruce, who built and lived in Kinross House, and

The stable-block at Kinross, built by Sir William Bruce before the house.
Note the circular doocot (centre).

William and Robert Adam, *père et fils*, the inventors of that consummate style of decoration that was afterwards adapted throughout the western world. Kinross House stands on the shores of Loch Leven, and the property was bought by Bruce following his completion of the restoration of Holyrood-house for the King, for which he received due monetary reward as well as a baronetcy. He chose the position carefully with an eye to planting the park before actually beginning any building; indeed, garden and grounds were already laid out and in a reasonable state of growth before the foundations of the house were completed. His son John was sent to France to learn courtly manners and also to bring back seeds of shrubs and trees, which he did in large number, and the bulk of these can still be seen lining the avenue from the town to the great mansion; "the most beautiful and regular piece of architecture in the kingdom", according to Daniel Defoe, and with a

The view of Loch Leven and its castle from the garden of Kinross House. It was from here that Mary, Queen of Scots, escaped in 1567.

garden "that makes Lady Lauderdale's at Ham but a wilderness in comparison".

Kinross House and garden are not much altered since they were finished and described in such glowing terms by contemporary visitors from the south, except for a stupid error made at the entrance, whereby the local authority has erected expensive but unsympathetic houses on either side of the gates, their bright red roofs clearly visible from the grey-slated house, a quarter of a mile away. This nullifies the comment that appeared in *A Tour thro' the Whole Island of Great Britain* in 1761, that "The Town lies at a leetle distance from the house so as not to obtrude upon its privacy and yet so as to be ready to wait upon its call." Bruce's original gates were replaced this century when Sir Basil Montgomery relaid the gardens to the old plan and renovated the house, which had stood empty for nearly a hundred years. Before that, one of the lairds, imbued with extreme Protestant fervour and a believer that all ornament was wicked, removed the gateposts and set about to deface the sculptured façade of the house. Happily he was stopped by the townspeople, and not long afterwards he was called to 'higher things'. Bruce himself was a notable respecter of local tradition and, unlike so many Palladian architects, retained evidences of past work wherever possible, incorporating them rather than demolishing them in his new designs. Thus Kinross House, one of the most patrician mansions in Britain, was provided with a superb vista of Loch Leven Castle from its garden side and with stables in the Scots vernacular on another, replete with ogee-roofed pavilions and circular doocot. Indeed the architect went further and incorporated a medieval carved stone from the castle in the arch of one of his garden gazebos, thus symbolizing the continuity of the feudal barony.

Bruce's apprentice as a young man was William Adam, father of the more celebrated Adam brothers, for one of whom, Robert, he bought the estate of Dowhill, with its ruined castle, which he renamed Blairadam. This was almost certainly in imitation of the 'master', and in later years William's grandson, Commissioner Adam, the man who introduced trial by jury into Scotland, was the guiding light in a local antiquarian society, a chief supporter of which was Sir Walter Scott. The latter found the key of Loch Leven Castle, wherein Mary, Queen of Scots had been kept prisoner and whence she escaped, and it went to Abbotsford after being shown to members of the Blairadam Society at one of their weekends in the Cleish Hills. It was from these hills, which divide Kinross-shire from Fife, that Bruce gained stone for his house, and no doubt William Adam too, though Blairadam never became the splendid mansion Kinross is, for 'Old Stone and Lime', as Adam *père* was called in the family, never got beyond enlarging what was in effect a rambling farmhouse, though he did build a hamlet at its gates, calling it Maryburgh, after his wife Mary Robertson; and he himself was styled 'of Maryburgh'.

The Cleish Hills are one of the best bits of Kinross-shire, with one or two nice lairds' towers and one village before either Fife or Clackmannan are reached, or Perthshire, which is normally entered through Glen Devon, at the northern end of which lies Strathearn and another world. Travellers will be familiar with Gleneagles, more properly Gleneagles Hotel, for when the Caledonian Railway came here, the laird of Gleneagles, the principal estate in the neighbourhood, permitted the use of the name on condition it was associated with the hotel. It has nothing to do with eagles, by the way, but derives from the Celtic word for a church and commemorates the early presence here of St Mungo, after whom a well on the estate is named and also the charming little private chapel. The house was about to be enlarged in the Bruce manner in the reign of William and Mary, but only a side pavilion and one or two adjuncts were ever completed, so that Gleneagles straggles somewhat and is not as comfortable as it might be; but it is pleasant just the same and in a superb setting, with the old ruined 'keep' of the Haldane lairds, who have been here over seven hundred years, standing nearer the road to the north. The present laird, the twenty-sixth, always flies his

Left. The Cleish Hills and a corner of the House of Aldie, recently restored in fulfilment of a boyhood dream by a Scotsman returned from exile.

The twenty-sixth Haldane laird of Gleneagles seen through a window of the ancient chapel from which his estate derives its name.

banner from it on Sundays.

Strathearn was a favourite resort of Celtic missionaries, St Fillan being the most frequent visitor and having a well-known village named after him. At Strathallan, in a mock-Gothic castle designed by Sir Robert Smirke, architect of the British Museum, Lady Roberts recently found part of a Celtic bell-cross in a drawer. It was the crucifix which would normally have been attached to the missionary bell, and she intended that it should go to a church, once the Museum of Antiquities in Edinburgh had disgorged it after a longish loan. Museums seem to have a habit of holding on to things in the hopes that the owners may forget or eventually make a gift of them, presumably on the assumption that they would look after them better. They have a case, but personally I think with Lady Roberts that religious works of art should be used for the purpose for which they were created, as near as possible, though perhaps being allowed out on loan for special exhibitions.

Possibly a place for Lady Roberts's Celtic bell-crucifix might be found in the former Collegiate Kirk at Tulliebardine, which was built before the Reformation and is unaltered since, being used as a burial-aisle of the Murray ancestors of the Duke of Atholl and in the care of Ancient Monuments. Elsewhere in Strathearn are the beautiful and well preserved saddle-back towers of Dunning and Muthill churches, the former now attached to a newer parish kirk but originally free-standing, as the one at Muthill and the cathedral *campanile* at Dunblane were. The area was evangelized by a sect known as 'the Culdees', a latter-day offshoot of the old Celtic missionaries surviving into the Romanized era and finally dying out, peacefully and more or less by agreement, in St Andrews. But Pictish towers (the finest in Scotland is at Abernethy) and Celtic shrines are typical of the region and give it a special character. They may even have developed from the settled conditions pertaining hereabouts following a long-standing Roman occupation. In any event, Strathearn has Roman remains of both roads and camps as well as an unusual number of Romanesque churches, many pre-dating the arrival of the Normans and their protective castles, and all within a few miles of Gleneagles Hotel and its celebrated golf course.

Apart from the Haldanes and the Murrays, there were also Drummonds established in this part of Perthshire in medieval times, the first of their number being said to have arrived with Margaret and Edgar Atheling, Saxon fugitives from William the Conqueror. A Drummond is said to have captained the ship bringing the future Queen and Saint to Scotland's shores – hence the wavy lines on the coat of arms. Be

The saddle-back tower of the kirk at Dunning, Strathearn – a good example of several in the neighbourhood, which was evangelized by Celtic monks.

this as it may, the Drummond seat stands on a rocky outcrop between Muthill and Crieff, on an ancient site, and their descendants still live *in situ*, albeit disguised as earls of Ancaster! Drummond Castle was the home of the Jacobite Duke of Perth, who with his sons and grandsons was forced to live abroad in the eighteenth century, the present Earl of Perth being only the second of that branch of the family to return to Scotland permanently, after the Earl of Ancaster had the happy idea of presenting him with Stobhall, a former dower-house, instead of handing it over to Ancient Monuments.

In the seventeenth century the gardens at Drummond were laid out by John Mylne, sixth master mason to six royal Stuart kings, and this formal arrangement was improved and enlarged in the nineteenth century for a visit by Queen Victoria, who was entertained in a huge marquee at the

centre. It is still a rather remarkable layout, especially when seen from the house, when all the coloured stones and florid patterns become more obvious. There was a lochan nearby, now drained, made artificially by a Jacobite Lady Perth in order to prevent Government troops encamping in the vicinity. We are here in strong Jacobite country; almost every house and town has played its part in the saga of the two unsuccessful attempts by the exiled Stuarts and their followers to reinstate themselves, and their subsequent loss of property, sometimes heads, titles and money. The Drummonds were the leaders in Perthshire, the Duke of Perth running what more or less amounted to a local press-gang to gain recruits for the cause. Their burial-place was across the Earn at Innerpeffray, where the old medieval kirk survives, replete with stone *mensa*, or table, and iron bars for windows. Beside it, overlooking a particularly attractive bend in the river, is the Innerpeffray Library, the first free library in Britain, founded by another Drummond, Lord Madderty, whose baronial pile stands empty and roofless in a field

*Left: An attractive
bend in the River
Earn viewed from
the library at
Innerpeffray near
Crieff.*

*Inside the library
at Innerpeffray.
This was the first
free public library
in the country and
contains many
famous works,
including Mon-
trose's Bible, in
French.*

nearby. This was not the first public library but the first free
one (the first was the cathedral library at Dunblane, founded
by Bishop Leighton a decade or so earlier), and its contents
are especially interesting, ranging from a copy of Raleigh's
History of the World to Montrose's Bible, in French, and
including works by William Drummond of Hawthornden
and Sir William Alexander of Menstrie as well as James VI
and I's *Blast against Tobacco*.

Lord Ancaster's mother-in-law was the indomitable Lady
Astor, the first woman to sit as a Member of Parliament. I

*Overleaf: Strathallan Castle, Auchterarder, viewed
from across the loch. This mock-Gothic residence was
designed by Sir Robert Smirke, architect of the
British Museum.*

was privileged to meet her at lunch one day and got on well with her despite his lordship's warning that I might not. Afterwards, when the next Conservative candidate for the division had to be chosen, it turned out to be Sir Alec Douglas-Home, now Lord Home again. Lord Ancaster suggested I should look through the library and see if I could find the record of the two Drummond sisters who were murdered and buried in Dunblane Cathedral in the reign of James IV, one of them having married that monarch and caused much embarrassment when an alliance was proposed between him and Margaret Tudor, sister of Henry VIII. The girls were poisoned, and it was only Lord Ancaster's retiring nature and respect for the present royal family that prevented his being more forthright and positive on the subject. Queen Victoria was not alone among regular royal visitors to Drummond: the Empress Eugénie stayed there often enough for her bedroom to be decorated with a plaster frieze composed of her and Napoleon III's busts. (In fact the Drummonds were related to the imperial couple through a son of Talleyrand; Louis-Napoleon's famous half-brother, the Duc de Morny, was similarly descended.) Charles X also visited Drummond, the last of the Bourbons and the one who "forgot nothing and learned nothing". Lady Astor used to sleep in his room and quite appreciated what might occur should the ghost of that 'bloody Bourbon' ever disturb her republican repose.

The Earn is, like Perthshire, only partially Lowland. Perth itself is a 'gateway to the Highlands', and much of the environs, notably to the north and west, are scarcely Lowland at all. The county used to stretch as far south as the Firth of Forth, as far west as the Trossachs, but this has now been taken away and placed in the Central Region, together with Dunblane and Doune, two very typical Perthshire places. Dunblane was the seat of the regional bishop, and Doune that of the earls of Moray and their Stewart ancestors. Raspberries grow at the Perthshire end of Strathmore, around Blairgowrie and Coupar Angus (which despite its name is not in Angus), as they do in the Carse of Gowrie, between Dundee

The cupola from the demolished House of Nairne, Sir William Bruce's last great work, now surmounting the James VI Hospital in Perth.

and the outskirts of Perth, and the city actually boasts a small port using the last bit of the tidal Tay. There is a certain loosening of Lowland primness in and around the town, which, however, has practically nothing of antiquity or real charm to show, little of real historical authenticity, not even the large Kirk of St John, first namesake of the burgh and still of its football team. Since Knox preached one of his most inflammatory sermons in St John's, the church has been several times restored, the most recent amounting almost to a rebuilding as a war-memorial to the dead of the First World War. As for the so-called 'Fair Maid's House', that has been so altered as to be virtually unrecognizable for what it once was, the headquarters of the medieval glovers' guild.

A place of mostly parallel streets, Perth does possess a few amusing souvenirs: the best are the Salutation Inn, where Prince Charlie stayed, and the cupola of the King James VI Hospital, which came from the House of Nairne. This was

The Jacobean rose and topiary garden at Stobhall, seat of the Earl of Perth and formerly a Drummond dower-house.

the last and finest of the mansions designed by Sir William Bruce, for the Nairnes, another Jacobite family. Lady Nairne was herself an architect of repute, perhaps the first lady architect, but she and her husband and sons and grandsons suffered exile, and in the end the property was put up for sale, when the Hanoverian Duke of Atholl, taking advantage of friends of the family who kept the bidding down to help the Nairnes get it back, deliberately sent the price up and thus acquired it. He then demolished the house and gave the cupola to the hospital in Perth, devastating the rest of the estate so that today nothing remains of what was once known as 'the glory of Strathord'. It lay to the west of the Tay, to the north of the city, not far from but on the opposite side to Stobhall, which is beautifully sited amongst woods on a high cliff above the river. This is only a small house which the Perths have made very comfortable, but it has a pre-Reformation chapel with a later ceiling painted with the arms and effigies of Charles I and his contemporaries, plus a small flat in which Ruskin and Millais resided, with their womenfolk (experimenting in wife-swapping at the time, with disastrous results). Poor Ruskin had been married at Bridgend, on the north side of the Tay, in Perth.

Perth has a bijou cathedral, seat of the Bishop of Dunkeld, Dunblane and St Andrews. It was designed in part by the gifted William Butterfield, and next door there used to be Queen's Barracks, home of the Black Watch, now demolished. The regiment has a museum and official headquarters in Hay Street, a name that recalls rivalry between the Hays and the Gowries for top Perth, as opposed to Perthshire, family. The burial-aisle of George Hay, first Earl of Kinnoull, is just across the river beneath Kinnoull Hill, the salubrious northern suburb of the city, where the hill itself has been crowned with a folly tower by a later earl with Wagnerian inclinations. The Tay is very fine at this point – no wonder the Romans admired it and compared it with the Tiber, though, as Scott remarked, their river is rather puny by comparison.

The town house of the Hays somehow got associated with the name Gowrie; it was subsequently called the Gowrie Inn and was unusual in being genuinely half-timbered, a thing one rarely finds in Scotland, but it was needlessly destroyed in the 1960s. The house was known as the place where the Gowrie Conspiracy to murder James VI came to a head; the King, however, managed to get to a top window and call for help, which arrived, and the Gowries in the building were all killed. Whether this is precisely what happened cannot be proved. James certainly wanted the Gowries out of the way, for one had participated in the murder of Rizzio, Mary, Queen of Scots' secretary, and another had arranged for the King's own kidnapping and shutting up in Gowrie Castle, since renamed Huntingtower. The royal youth escaped by asking to go hunting and, having a good memory, got his own back either by design or chance in that fracas in the Gowrie House in Perth.

Perth has a fine eighteenth-century bridge over the Tay, designed by John Smeaton, who built one over the Deveron at Banff and an almost exactly similar one over the Tweed at Coldstream, the one at Perth replacing John Mylne's. A second, newer bridge was opened by the Queen a few years ago, and now the Tay is crossed at a high level by a motorway bridge which gives splendid views of the city and surroundings towards both the Highlands and the sea. Then there are the Inches, not really islands but a big and a slightly smaller oasis of grass and trees on the larger of which took place that legendary clan fight described by Scott in *The Fair Maid*; facing it is a not uncomplementary version of Adam's north side of Charlotte Square in Edinburgh, replete with sphinxes on the end pavilions. On the whole, Perth is better in its surroundings than in itself, as is so often the case with Scottish towns, and it relies mainly on whisky, dyeworks and tourism to keep going. It has none of the dramatic appeal of Stirling, whose site is probably amongst the best of all Scottish burghs, with castle rising magnificently from the plain, edged with both Highland and Lowland hills and the green valley of the Forth running through.

The Tay is a larger river and has more noble seats along its banks, claiming at Meikleour the tallest and longest beech hedge in the world. Scone, of course, is near Perth; it was built by Lord Mansfield, descendant of the great Lord Chief Justice of England, who employed William Atkinson as his architect, the same whom the Bard of Abbotsford consulted but later discarded. He found he could do the thing himself, more or less, and get the curiously romantic effect we see today, which no architect could, or probably would wish to have produced. Atkinson was asked by Lord Mansfield to keep a portion of the old palace of the kings of Scots and what remained of the monastery whence the monks were supposed to have handed Edward I the 'Stone of Destiny'. (It is a moot point if they actually did this and may not have fobbed off the

The Mercat Cross, Meikleour, Perthshire. Meikleour is better known for its immense beech hedge, but this is a rare example of an unspoilt pre-Reformation Cross in Scotland.

arrogant Plantagenet with a piece of local sandstone in place of the limestone talisman which our mythical ancestors were said to have brought here from the Near East, via Ireland, and which they claimed was 'Jacob's pillow'.) In practice Atkinson did not much respect what was left of the past at Scone but built a new Tudorized-Gothic structure and almost all of substance that has survived is an old gateway standing otiose in the park. It was the port of the burgh in whose kirk Charles II suffered a two-hour harangue from a Covenanting preacher before being crowned by the Earl of Argyll, then marquis, the one who personally assisted in the destruction of Airlie Castle and had Montrose killed. A contemporary account describes the exhortation as "something lairge", and the occasion was the last on which the 'Honours of Scotland' were used before being put in the safe-keeping of the Knight Marischal at Dunnottar, rescued and then used until 1707 for the Riding of the Scottish Parliament. They were locked away in an oak kist after this and lay forgotten until Sir Walter Scott found them safe and sound where they had been put more than a century earlier.

The south-western end of Perthshire has been wrenched away from it and added to the Central Region, which includes quite a lot of the Highlands and the whole valley of the Forth, with its chief tributary the Teith. This flows out of Loch Katrine and reaches the Forth near Dunblane, where the small but exquisite cathedral was Ruskin's favourite – "No common man built Dunblane," he said. It is Early English at its best and purest, and although the choir has been heavily restored inside, by Lorimer, the rest was sympathetically renovated earlier by Sir Rowand Anderson and must be counted amongst the most successful rejuvenations of an important pre-Reformation church in Scotland. It did not escape the religious upheavals of the sixteenth and seventeenth centuries unharmed – only Glasgow can claim that amongst Scottish mainland cathedrals, but it looks authentic outside, and the interior of the nave is so. The tower is older and belongs to that group of Romanesque free-standing bell-towers of which Muthill's and Dunning's have already been mentioned. It does, perhaps, form a link with the Culdees, and Dunblane itself recalls the possibility of a Celtic foundation for its pre-Norman cathedral, St Blane having come from Ireland, via Rome, and died here. Dunblane hydro may also have older origins, for there is said to have been a well there dedicated to St Ronan.

Nearby Bridge of Allan is a spa as well, and between the two is the site of the Field of Sheriffmuir, where an inconclusive battle was fought between the supporters of 'The King over the Water', led by the Earl of Mar, and of George I, led by the Duke of Argyll. Mar could easily have won but for some reason or another stopped half-way and went into consultation, and both parties left the battlefield without any more fighting. (It seems that neither was keen on shedding blood and so, having demonstrated their respective positions, retired. The event has certainly never been satisfactorily explained.) Doune Castle is the most interesting old building hereabouts, the surroundings being otherwise dominated by

Dunblane Cathedral from the east, showing the restored choir and fine cam-panile, Romanesque at the foot, fortified Gothic above.

the distant prospect of Stirling and the nearer Wallace Memo-rial on Abbey Craig. Doune is perhaps the best of all the fifteenth- and earlier-century castles in Scotland since it is neither restored nor ruined but roofed and repaired as Ruskin and Samuel Butler would have approved. The former hated what he called "emergent ruins from a shaven lawn", while the latter thought old buildings should be allowed to decay gently, though not to fall down. One might add that Doune is a smaller version of a castle of *enceinte*, one with all its parts ranged around an outer wall and lacking a central redoubt, on the model of Pierrefonds, which Viollet-le-Duc rebuilt for Napoleon III in the forest of Compiègne.

Doune should be seen by the passing traveller from the bridge over the Teith, on the south side of the tiny village, with its fine mercat cross and memories of Doune pistols,

'Queen Mary's Bower' at the priory of Inchmahome on the lake of Menteith, Perthshire. The tall box trees are said to be overgrown hedges planted by the infant Mary, Queen of Scots, in 1547.

which were made there. Beyond, one senses the approach of the Highlands and so passes out of this 'View', though one may perhaps mention Doune Lodge and Lord Moray's Motor Museum and perhaps include the Lake of Menteith, Scotland's only lake as opposed to loch, its very name being Lowland rather than Highland.

The Lake of Menteith is well known to holidaymakers, with an hotel and little port for fishermen and people who like boats. In the middle is Inchmahome, the island whence Mary, Queen of Scots, left with her four Maries and half-brother for France, there to be brought up in the safety and sophisticated atmosphere of the French Court. She planted a garden on the island which may or may not be represented in 'Queen Mary's Bower', an unruly collection of box hedges grown to shrub dimensions, the whole suggesting paths and edging on quite a different scale. She must have lived in the priory,

All that remains of Cambuskenneth Abbey, burial-place of James III of Scots and his queen, Margaret of Denmark.

which then still flourished and was under royal patronage, its church containing the tombs of the Stewarts and their ancestors, one particular tomb being unique in Christendom in its merging of Celtic and Gothic sculpture and symbolism. It shows a recumbent Stewart knight in full armour with his spouse in flowing robes, the two leaning towards one another as if to embrace. Menteith was not despoiled at the Reformation, at least not by religious despoilers, its site obviously being somewhat inhibiting for the iconoclasts lying in the middle of a lake; the stones were removed later by the earls of Mar, who acquired the temporal lordships of the Priory of Inchmahome and the Abbey of Cambuskenneth, near Stirling, and who made the best use they could of the building-materials available.

Cambuskenneth, a royal establishment, was built by one of the Mylnes, who acted as both canon and mason and was the ancestor of that family which was responsible for bridges, abbeys and palaces in different parts of Scotland in the fifteenth, sixteenth and seventeenth centuries. In it was buried Mylne's sovereign, the ill-fated James III, who, though girded with the sword of Bruce and mounted on a mighty charger, took fright during the Battle of Sauchieburn and rode off, only to collapse near a farmhouse where he was murdered by a noble posing as a priest. The abbey of Cambuskenneth stood ready at hand to receive his body, which it duly did, as well as that of his queen, Margaret of Denmark, in whose wake Orkney and Shetland came to Scotland. At the Reformation the destruction here was considerable, and the only substantial item left by a combination of 'deformers', vandals and secular abbots was the free-standing *campanile* we see today. The royal tombs were desecrated and not restored until Queen Victoria ordered that the tombs of her Scottish ancestors be reconstructed and put back where they had originally been. The abbey, set on a flat carse between a winding and twisting Forth, is now in the care of Ancient Monuments. It has its place in the view from the castle at Stirling with the grander, more ostentatiously sited Wallace Memorial, but it is just as fine even in ruin as that extraordinary object.

Too big, with no fixed shape and neither a tower nor a proper memorial but a mixture, with an enlarged version of the crown of St Giles High Kirk in Edinburgh on top, the design of the Wallace Memorial was at first simpler and less eclectic, but the nineteenth century being what it was, this, a more ornate, second design, was undertaken. The architect was J.T. Rochhead, who is commemorated in a small park in Edinburgh and was the creator of Minard Castle, in Argyll, which latter, possibly on the site of an older structure, shows some of the same decorative propensities as the Wallace Memorial but in a different style. Signs of changed times in our century may be recalled in the fact that Wallace's sword was stolen and that nationalism today expresses itself in a Scottish Nationalist Provost of Stirling, one who, I am glad

The Wallace Memorial crowning Abbey Craig, Airthrey – the view from the former park, now the campus of Stirling University.

to say, stood up for the Queen and her loyal subjects when students of the University at Airthrey insulted Her Majesty and got some support from sycophantic lecturers. The whole episode was a disgrace not only to Stirling and its new seat of learning but to Scotland, and although some of the letters received by the offending students and their adult hangers-on verged on the obscene, and others were rather wild in tone, I do not think any of the offenders will forget the incident or say much about it to their posterity.

Stirling University covers much of the former Airthrey Estate, just below the Wallace Memorial and on the north side of the Forth; and Airthrey itself was laid out and the mansion built from drawings by Robert Adam. It was a Haldane property, and the laird at that time behaved in a distinctly unsatisfactory manner, obtaining the architect's plans and then employing an estate builder to carry them out, giving Robert Adam small credit for his splendid scheme. It was one of the first and best essays in his new castellated style, of which Culzean, on the Ayrshire coast, is the better known. The Haldanes, for there were two brothers, then went on to romanticize the park and actually advertised for a hermit to inhabit the rustic Gothic cell they had erected for him – and they got

one for a while. They were pamphleteers, religious tractarians of the most virulent and typical British kind, spread-
ing their tentacles abroad, even to India, yet somehow
knowing what to do architecturally, enough to carry out the
suggestions of the greatest master of the age without further
consultation beyond studying the plans they had received. In
the nineteenth century the Haldane version of an Adam castle
was baronialized by a Glasgow businessman, the result
plainly showing how much better the eighteenth century was
in almost every respect when it came to taste and *savoir faire*.

The second half of the twentieth century has seen an improvement in cultural matters, perhaps because we have
begun to realize what we are losing with so many demolitions
and changes that we hardly know where we are. Left-wing
politicians are attacking us in one direction, anxious to
'change society' and, therefore, not averse to the destruction
of the existing environment, while intellectuals generally
tend to assist in the process, albeit not always on purpose. It
has now gone as far as I think it will, and already there is a
swing in the opposite direction, perhaps too much of one,
with excessive snooping by Preservation and Amenity
Societies, often led by well-meaning amateurs, who are permitted by new legislation to examine any plan or scheme put
up by private individuals and not only to comment on it but
possibly to prevent its execution. One has heard of alarming
interferences, such as a friend who was temporarily stopped
from converting the basement of his house to his own use
because some busybody did not like the new door-knobs. In
fact, they were original Georgian ones!

The biggest change for the better has occurred in towns
outside Edinburgh, such as Stirling. Indeed, it was there, as
part of the festival they have in May, that I gave a lecture on
Sir William Bruce in the old Tolbooth, which he designed,
and whilst there I visited a decayed building at the top of the
same street with a local official. It is called 'Mar's Wark', and I
was informed that the building was "a load of rubbish and
ought to be demolished". Since then that particular official,

Mar's Wark – detail of Renaissance sculpture. This building, never finished, was begun by the Keeper of Stirling Castle in Jacobean times in imitation of the royal example.

and many others of like mind, have jumped on the preservation band-waggon, and it would be a bold man, official or not, who would now repeat what he said about 'Mar's Wark' or any similar structure. Only the façade of this building has survived, or was probably ever completed; it is wildly extravagant and foreign-looking and was the work of that Earl of Mar who despoiled Cambuskenneth. He must have been trying to emulate the King at the castle, and especially the palace block which was built by French and Flemish masons. Certainly 'Mar's Wark' is covered with rich Renaissance ornament, misunderstood and almost Gothic in feeling, so barbarous is it, but it should not be pulled down. On the opposite side of the road, or nearly so, is Argyll's Lodging, the finest truly Renaissance town house in Scotland. It was built for Sir William Alexander of Menstrie, Earl of Stirling

119

The fifteenth-century Stirling Brig, one of the finest in Scotland
Forth a

e one after which the battle was named, which was higher up the
timber.

and Viscount Canada under Charles I. Beyond is the castle whose site so closely resembles that of Edinburgh, except that its rock stands out more sharply from the plain, and it has been less modernized to accommodate soldiers.

At the end of the last war it was proposed as a suitable war-memorial to those who gave their lives to defeat Hitler, that Stirling Castle should finally be wrested from the Army and restored. The plan fell through, but something has been achieved: the fifteenth-century Great Hall is in the process of renovation, and the former Chapel Royal, once used as a dance-hall by the Argylls, has been redecorated and opened to the public. Other works continue, and the Army are gradually being pushed out. One has to 'gang warily' in such matters; indeed, success often depends on some chance happening, such as when a carved wooden roundel fell from the ceiling of the King's Chamber onto the head of a soldier some years ago, revealing a whole set of similar items – Renaissance effigies of kings and queens, Roman emperors, Jewish

Left: Stirling Castle viewed from the west, showing in the foreground the King's Knott, a series of terraces formerly planted, now only grass.

An iron yett, or gate, at the side entrance over the fosse, or moat, of Stirling Castle.

prophets and kings, Greek and Roman heroes and Italian cherubs. Most of them have since been rescued and have been on view in the Smith Institute in Stirling or in the Museum of Antiquities in Edinburgh prior to re-instatement in the castle.

From the castle, of course, one can see everything: the Wallace Memorial against its almost Highland background, the Forth flowing down from the slopes of Ben Lomond to become, after a series of serpent-like twists, wide and tidal. There is Cambuskenneth amidst the first contortions, then the Kincardine Bridge and finally the sea. One can make out Stirling Brig, not the one where the battle was so hardly won

The sculptor C. d'O. Pilkington Jackson's masterpiece, an equestrian Robert Bruce on the Field of Bannockburn.

by William Wallace long ago – that was built of timber and was in a different position – but the beautiful three-arched stone bridge dating from the fifteenth century. It is one of the finest in a country famous for its bridges, and has now been pedestrianized and isolated. On the other side of Stirling, in a south-westerly direction, are the Fintry Hills and the Buchanan country at the southern end of Loch Lomond, so to Glasgow and its purlieus. The view towards the south is filled by the Field of Bannockburn, now organized as a showplace and set with C. d'O. Pilkington Jackson's last and most important creation, his bronze equestrian statue of Robert the Bruce. The King is helmeted so that one cannot really see what he looks like, but the sculptor swore he had got the shape from an authentic skull, the skull of a sensitive, small man, almost feminine, and said to resemble the one found under the floor of the ruined abbey at Dunfermline. To me this does not matter too much, for the result is splendid and inspiring and the artist's masterpiece.

There is a less controversial statue of Bruce on the castle esplanade, surrounded by a protective ring of symbolic caltrops, the iron spikes that helped to win the day at Bannockburn. It is rather feeble by comparison with Pilkington Jackson's. Then there are two statues in Edinburgh, one on either side of the castle entrance, of Bruce and Wallace respectively. Their story was told me by the late John Matthew, Sir Robert Lorimer's partner, when I was last chief assistant in that famous office. Apparently the sculptor in this case was 'pinkish' in politics, a man who would not stand up for the National Anthem, yet it was he who insisted that the model for Bruce should be a nobleman, while that for Wallace should be a 'man of the people'. Actually Wallace was a knight and a gentleman, and Bruce a feudal baron, but the idea was reasonable and the resulting contrast successful. Wallace, incidentally, bears on his shield the Scottish saltire, and Bruce the rampant lion, which is absolutely correct, the latter being the royal banner and the private property of the sovereign, the former the national device of Scotland and available to us all. The dichotomy between the two characters is interesting and is reflected in the Scottish attitude towards other national heroes – Burns and Scott, for example, the 'Poet of the Plough' and the Laird of Abbotsford, though here again the real differences were much less than some would have us believe.

Stirling was for long the capital of Scotland and probably would have remained so had it not been too far from the sources of power after 1603 and the Union of the Crowns. Edinburgh finally became Scotland's chief city in 1633 when Charles I was crowned at Holyrood. Before then the capital was wherever the Court happened to be, and its presence brought considerable kudos and trade to everyone concerned. James VI used to hold the threat of moving from, say, Edinburgh to Stirling whenever his nobles, lawyers and creditors became obstreperous and on one occasion actually did move,

The house of James IV's tailor in the old town of Stirling. The Scottish Court was for centuries established here, and all the way up to the castle are numerous houses dating from the fifteenth to seventeenth century.

which meant that they all had either to travel daily to attend him or to acquire new lodgings for themselves. The King organized the christening of his eldest boy, Henry, at Stirling, when the Chapel Royal where he himself had been baptized was renovated; and his own mother had been crowned in the Kirk of the Halyrude, so there were good precedents for Stirling's high position – a position lost with the departure of the Stewarts and the setting-up of a mere garrison in the royal castle in place of a Court. The site, on the other hand, remains superb, without equal in the United Kingdom, and, having witnessed Scotland's greatest victory in the fight to establish herself as a separate entity, the town must inevitably keep its particular place in history.

Until recently, when the inhabitants of Stirling elected a Scottish Nationalist Provost and gave the Socialists a nasty fright in the Parliamentary elections, they had not shown any special aggressiveness or excessive local pride; the young men had decently cut hair, and the place seemed less brash and sophisticated than Edinburgh and other cities. Then a Festival was started, and a really first-class restaurant opened, where one could get dinner in the evening instead of just high tea. So civilization advanced, with a university as well, and now there are motorways all over the place, more especially to Glasgow, where it is obvious the shoppers go and not to Edinburgh, whose dual carriageway is almost pristine by comparison. This is the most gentle of motorways, the one from Stirling to the capital; from it one sees a great deal of the country without too much harassment by fast or heavy commercial traffic; it is the quietest and pleasantest motorway I know; and now the last, long-delayed link has been forged, crossing that curious piece of *terra incognita* between Stirling and Airth. The area is absolutely flat, a repetition of the Low Countries atmosphere on the north bank of the Forth, and so very un-Scottish as to be almost unreal. One can run down to the Forth's edge at South Alloa, where there used to be a ferry and still is a pier, and study the mixture of high hills and wide-flowing river, factories and smoke, and flat meadows to one's heart's content. There are some pleasant white farmhouses to be glimpsed either at close quarters or as one drives along the motorway, and at Airth a slight rise in the contours marks the site of Airth Castle, Gothic-Revival and also partly ancient, complementary to Clackmannan tower immediately opposite.

Airth is now an hotel, while Dunmore Park, a little further 'inland', stands empty, though its estate is still farmed. In the grounds is Scotland's most amusing and imaginatively conceived folly, which takes the form of a giant pineapple, the protruding stone leaves being held in position by iron stays. It marked the principal feature of the hot-houses and was probably the work of Sir William Chambers, rival to the Adam brothers for fame and commissions in the second half of the eighteenth century. He was a great favourite of George III, who disliked Robert Adam and the Pompeian décor he propagated, preferring the more solid Palladian taste adopted by Chambers. Indeed, he employed him as tutor to his chil-

Scotland's most distinguished folly, 'The Pineapple' at Dunmore, near Airth. This was the centrepiece of the hot-houses. The projecting stone leaves are held in place by iron stays.

dren. Chambers was of Scots parentage but born in Stockholm, whence he was taken to China – hence perhaps his interest in chinoiserie; he introduced Chinese modes into Britain and, through his French friends, onto the Continent. The Dunmore Pineapple forms part of a special holiday-centre run by the Landmark Trust, which specializes in unusual sites and can often arrange for one to stay in a folly or pavilion, though not this one.

From Airth one must either cross the river into Fife or go to Glasgow or Edinburgh, in which latter case the new motorway calls. Perhaps one might give a backward glance in the direction of Falkirk and spare a thought for the Carron Works, which made the guns to defeat Napoleon and other foes and whose elegant Regency grates are now much sought-after by collectors. The landscape is still Netherlandish until one has passed Grangemouth oil-refineries and reached the hills on the south side of the Forth and the line of the old Roman Wall, the one built by Antoninus and still perceivable in places. The *vallum*, or ditch, runs right in front of Callendar Park, the great empty mansion that recalls a French *château* and was the place where the marriage contract between François II of France and Mary, Queen of Scots was signed. At the sale of contents, some valuable and interesting objects were obtainable for prices that would make modern addicts green with envy. Charles X of France often stayed at Callendar Park, and the salon was full of handsome blue-and-gold French furniture. The Provost of Falkirk at the time said he would like the house demolished; it reminded him, he said, "of the days of serfdom". It is certainly very large, but surely any association with serfdom is an exaggeration? Even in Russia, where they had serfdom, the Communists have not pulled down old or historic buildings; rather they have restored them expensively and turned them into tourist-attractions. In any event, the mansion still survives, gloomily empty in its dark, wooded setting, the park partly used for housing and official purposes, its centrepiece waiting till someone has an idea what to do with it.

Roslin Glen at Hawthornden, a favourite walk of Scott and many others, including the Wordsworths and, of course, the poet William Drummond.

CHAPTER FOUR

LOTHIAN, EDINBURGH AND THE BORDERS

IT USED to be said that the folk from East Lothian were brighter than those from West Lothian because they went to market, in Edinburgh, with the sun behind them and returned in the evening similarly guided, while their opposite numbers had the sun in their faces both ways. Be that as it may, East Lothian has a gayer reputation than West Lothian, which is more industrialized, less attractive scenically and generally not so popular. Yet it contains Linlithgow with its magnificent Royal Palace, once the pride of Scotland, the birthplace of Mary, Queen of Scots, and adjoining is St Michael's Collegiate Kirk, perhaps the finest of the old burgh churches built shortly before the Reformation. The surroundings are not the most salubrious in the country, though they have been improved greatly recently, and the group of palace, kirk and town hall at Linlithgow, mirrored in the loch on good days, is now seen to advantage from the Stirling-to-Edinburgh motorway. From it, West Lothian no longer seems especially grubby; true, there are still a few shale oil-bings, or heaps, but most of these have been levelled and 'landscaped', turned into grass and planted with shrubs, so that the effect is almost natural. As a matter of fact, in the old days the pinkish, orange shades of the bings, particularly at sunset, were not unpleasant, though there was usually a bit of a smell, and, lacking any soil, nothing much would grow except fireweed.

*The industrial landscape near Blackburn, West Lothian – former elegance
backed by shale oil-bings.*

Linlithgow town has had a face-lift since the war, not all of
it successful or necessary. I have already referred to the comments of at least one provost of a Lowland burgh and really
cannot refrain from quoting another. When there was opposition to the demolition of some fine upstanding old Scots
buildings opposite the town hall, on the way up to the kirk
and palace, we the protesters were told by the provost that
they did not want "another Pompeii" in Linlithgow. Of
course, no one wanted that, and now there is no chance of it,
for almost everything has gone, except the largest and most
difficult structures to move, the seventeenth-century Town
House, designed by Robert Mylne, the semi-ruined palace
and the former collegiate kirk. This latter had a crown-steeple
of the same kind that still tops St Giles High Kirk in Edinburgh and King's College Chapel in Aberdeen and also once
crowned St Mary's Kirk in Haddington, but that, with the
one in Linlithgow, was taken down because it was said to be

The palace and kirk at Linlithgow viewed from across the loch. The birth-place of Mary, Queen of Scots, the palace survived intact until accidentally burned in 1745.

dangerous. Recently a simplified and somewhat spiky replica has been hoisted onto St Michael's Tower. Few like it, but I will refrain from adverse comment because its erection does show a constructive turn of mind, and if the new 'crown' is not to everyone's taste, it is well meant. So much has been needlessly removed both here and in other parts of Scotland that the opposite example makes a welcome change, especially when the rebuilding approximates in some degree to what went before.

Behind Linlithgow, to the south, are the Binny Hills, a remarkable outcrop of volcanic scenery with a famous hill fort on the highest point. Much of central Scotland can be seen from there; indeed, on a clear day the view stretches practically right across the country, from Ben Lomond to Berwick Law. The Forth can be seen as in an air-photo, widening towards the sea, with both the bridges, the triple-cantilevered railway one, which for me is the more exciting and beautiful, and the new suspension road-bridge. All around is that mixed landscape of factories, slag-heaps and greenery that is typical of the central Lowlands. It is the most populated area after Clydeside and was almost totally devastated in the nineteenth century by too hasty development and sheer greed, with little thought for posterity or the conditions of life thereby created. We have been reaping the results ever since, with run-down works, loss of jobs and a semi-twilight environment, not to mention the problem of finding new economic outlets and new homes. The 'new town' of Livingston is a specific outcome of this, spick and span but without a heart, so far, well designed and laid out but yet to find its feet or prove the right answer. It does not purvey the same air of prosperity and belief in the future one finds in modern Aberdeen, which was a more natural growth, even if the oil may give out before the century is over. We must learn that nothing is static, that not only do means of livelihood and the places in which we live change, but the whole method of existence, transport included. One thinks, for instance, of the canals that once criss-crossed the Lowlands and which are now mostly dried up or weedy, of the coal that was transported along them and which fired the furnaces that drove the machines. It is now at a discount *vis-à-vis* other motive-powers, and much of the population is either unemployed or has gone to find more agreeable work elsewhere.

In the process of tidying up, the entire scene has become improved in a remarkably short space of time, and one has come to realize as never before that, despite so much industry, West Lothian possesses a surprising amount of good agricultural land, a number of fine wooded parks and some interesting architectural mementos of a more distant past. The county boasts an unusual number of old kirks; indeed, Ian Lindsay, who lived in a typical West Lothian laird's tower, at Houston, brought out a series of 'wee bookies' on them, including the one at Strathbrock where he had the laird's pew. The best is probably at Abercorn, on a

A group of typical Lowland houses at Linlithgow. These douce 'biggins', with forestairs, whitewashed walls and red pantiles are now disappearing fast.

hill above the Firth of Forth, near the site of a Roman fort in the grounds of Hopetoun House. There was a Pictish monastery there, and attached to the medieval church are two aisles, or family burial-chapels, of the Hopes, of whom more anon, and of the Dalyells, one of whose modern representatives is the local Member of Parliament. His ancestor was the notorious Tam Dalyell, the Cavalier who went to Russia rather than live under Cromwell and who returned at the King's restoration a general in the Tsar's army. It was he who founded the Scots Greys, the 'white' busby of their ceremonial kit recalling the winter regalia worn in Russia. Tam was much feared by the Covenanters, who told stories of how he 'supped with the Devil', and in the park at The Binns, his old home, there used to be a marble table-top which he is said to have thrown at the Devil when he cheated at cards, or some such legend.

The Hopes, whose aisle at Abercorn is the larger and more important, and the one still used on Sundays, takes the dual form of burial-aisle and 'opera-box', the latter situated high above the congregation at the east end, and possibly a little embarrassing for those who sit there, who are 'on show', so to speak. The family emanated from Fife and acquired their West Lothian estates in the reign of Charles II, one of their number being created Earl of Hopetoun in the stead of his father, who was drowned whilst trying to save James, Duke of York, brother of the King, from drowning. Hopetoun House, which was begun shortly afterwards, was designed by Sir William Bruce and continued and enlarged by his apprentice William Adam, and the Adam brothers, over a period of a hundred years, when it became what has been called 'the Versailles of Scotland'. Here George IV was entertained in 1822 and in more modern times lived the Marquis of Linlithgow, Viceroy of India. The view eastwards from the main front takes in both road and railway bridges and is, perhaps, symbolic of the varied character of the county, with the naval dockyard just across the Firth of Forth at Rosyth and Port Edgar almost at the entrance-gates. The great house is now only partially the home of the Linlithgows, who have made the property into a trust, their collection of paintings and furniture brought together by their forebears, and some of it, by James Adam, being open regularly to the public and safe, presumably, from dispersal or sale.

At South Queensferry, between the bridges, is the one Carmelite friary kirk in Great Britain still used as a place of worship. Only a portion of the building survives; it does so because it was created under the patronage of the local laird and became his private chapel at the Reformation – otherwise it would have gone. It stands by the water's edge in this salty little burgh, a place which, having largely lost its trade through the building of the bridges and the ending of the ferry, enjoys a sort of Indian summer as a minor tourist-resort, near enough Edinburgh to attract visitors in cars and buses during the Festival. It has one snag, however, as I discovered when recommending the local inn to friends as somewhere to stay instead of the capital: I had forgotten the railway bridge and the noise of the trains crossing and recrossing on the 'iron way' – they did not sleep much that night; and the little town is somewhat overshadowed by the new road bridge, whose concrete approach-arches cover part of it. Still, it is a pleasant enough spot, with the disused harbour finding rejuvenation as a 'marina', and fish-restaurants doing well.

The waters of the tidal Forth are already pretty filthy by the time South Queensferry is reached; sea-life is at a minimum in a region where oysters were once plentiful, and just beyond the railway bridge, the real Forth Bridge, is an artificial island created as a berthing for oil-tankers. The woods at Dalmeny, seat of the Roseberys, come right down to the sea, and there is a public footpath along to Cramond, an old Roman camp and now almost part of Edinburgh. A seafront esplanade runs along the shore to the outskirts of the city, and if one knows the way through Granton Docks to Leith, a whole new world unfamiliar to many 'Edimbourgeois' and most visitors opens. It is lively, a little untidy but pleasantly so, and includes a restored fishermen's settlement at Newhaven, whence the celebrated fisherwives came with the 'Caller Herrin' in baskets from door to door. On special occasions they used to wear their colourful red-striped costumes, now a gala dress, but when I saw them they mostly appeared in navy blue.

Leith has similarities with Genoa. It is hard to explain this, but friends who know that Ligurian city agree with me about it. It may be because of its less well ordered, less respectable, more workaday air as compared with the capital, and its position as a port and wine-depot. Some of the warehouses are of considerable antiquity, and the story is told of how the Duke of Albany, in the fifteenth century, made his escape to France in a wine-cask after getting his jailers drunk. One firm still functioning, Cockburn's of Leith, was founded by Robert Cockburn, brother of Henry, Lord Cockburn, whose *Memorials* describe life in Edinburgh and its environs during the great flitting from the Old Town to the New at the end of the

Above: The plaque on the quayside at Leith marking the spot where George IV landed in 1822. Right: The view through the port of Monk's Citadel at Leith – the site has now nearly been cleared.

eighteenth century, and the period of settling-in early in the nineteenth. Anyway, the Continental feeling is there, and the skyscrapers, one known as 'the Banana' on account of its curved shape, add to the illusion. There is also a considerable area of no-man's land in Leith, demolished sites not yet entirely re-covered with buildings, and in one such stands a tiny remnant of General Monk's Citadel, a port, or entry-gate.

Leith has had its great days. It was formerly independent of Edinburgh, and its decline almost certainly dates from incorporation in and swallowing up by the capital. In 1822, however, George IV landed at Leith, almost at the same spot as Mary, Queen of Scots some 250 years earlier, and a plaque marks the place. It was the first time a monarch of the Hanoverian line had set foot in North Britain, and Scott did what he could to make the occasion as colourful and romantic and, I am bound to say, hilarious as possible. Tartans came out in a rash – even the King and the Lord Mayor of London donned the kilt, the King with silk tights beneath; but Scott never fell for that, not even for the tartan the Galashiels woollen-merchants tried to foist on him: a black-and-white shepherd's plaid was all he ever sported, and that over his shoulder. The entire event was faintly ridiculous, bordering on the improper, though our present system of clans and tartans pertaining

thereto mostly dates from this extraordinary occasion. Until then lairds and nobles in the Lowlands would almost rather have been seen dead than in Gaelic garb, while even in the Highlands the kilt was not the habitual dress of the gentry, who rode horses and wore trews. Now all is changed; the ghillies wear trousers, and the gentry tend to appear in the kilt.

In writing about Stirling I mentioned that it was only in the reign of Charles I that Edinburgh officially became the capital of Scotland. In fact, Leith was mooted as a suitable chief city before that and for a while had a chance of being chosen. Charles himself liked the place and was often to be seen playing a game of golf on its links. His son James, Duke of York, won a match over some southern contenders when he took for partner one Jock Paterson; and when the proceeds were halved, Jock built 'Golfer's Land' in the Canongate, a fine old house not long since demolished. Leith also got a number of good neo-Classical public buildings in Regency times designed by some of the same architects as Edinburgh's New Town. They survive but with different functions, amidst warehouses and offices, together with a much earlier neighbour, Lamb's House. This was the building in which Andrew Lamb hosted Mary, Queen of Scots when she landed nearby, in what Knox described as a "well deserved" haar, or sea fog.

Leith has been made by those who refuse to construct a proper bypass round Edinburgh into a 'thruway' for traffic from the west making for the East Lothian resorts and the A1 to Berwick, which road continues through Portobello and Musselburgh via further bottlenecks before emerging on a slightly less crowded part of the main road south. The A1 actually begins in Princes Street. I know something about this as I was the person principally concerned in organizing the opposition to a concrete roundabout in Randolph Crescent, where I live, and the cutting down of the trees in our gardens and adjoining ones in order to make a new bus- and lorry-route through the predominantly residential parts of the city rather than divert heavy traffic away from it. The day was won, and the best of the Georgian New Town was saved; today the threat seems to have evaporated. The buses never came, the gardens remain, and we do not have concrete gibbets for lamp-posts; but the lorries do come and, since the opening of the Forth Road Bridge, have been getting bigger and heavier all the time, rattling the buildings day and night and making it virtually impossible to sleep without double glazing, and even difficult then. Complaints to local councillors are almost useless, since the responsibility is as much that of the Region as of the District, who do not agree and are of different political complexions. So we continue to suffer. It really is curious that Edinburgh, the capital of Scotland, cannot or will not do anything to control the passage of heavy lorries through the city. Almost every other place of standing, including Glasgow, prohibits such traffic at the centre, and on the Continent every small village sends the *poids lourds* round the outside, but not Edinburgh, where they seem to think they might lose trade by taking action on this matter.

One of the happiest fashions of the nineteenth century was the addiction to coloured prints of picturesque views in which Edinburgh, 'the Athens of the North', offered itself, as perhaps no other city in the kingdom, to the engravers and lithographers. The taste even spread to France, where *vues pittoresques d'Edimbourg* could be seen decorating music-sheets, novel-covers and all sorts of things. Naturally, all visitors have seen the castle from Princes Street, that "jolly view" as one inmate of the august New Club used to say when taking guests to coffee upstairs – and so it is. Unfortunately, the old first-floor tea-rooms which were such a delight in the past have moved behind into the side streets, where there is practically no view at all, never mind a jolly one; and apart from clubs and a few showrooms, that unique aspect of 'Auld Reekie' has been largely lost. As for the street itself, that is commonplace and probably always was, despite the cries of horror whenever a new store or standardized façade is erected. It has always been pretty dull during my lifetime, if not positively ugly. Probably the rot started when the regulations controlling height and size of buildings were relaxed, at the beginning of this century; but Princes Street still has no neon signs on its shop-fronts, many of which might almost be improved by them, and it is not many years since a letter appeared in the Press deploring the arrival of the 'Continental Sunday' and the prospect of lemonade being sold to visitors in the gardens on a Sabbath morn.

Lord Cockburn, 'Cocky', who founded Britain's first amenity society, thought Princes Street amongst the meanest in the United Kingdom, and this being so, one wonders on what grounds, other than the superb view, it ever acquired the superior cachet some people attach to it. It is one-sided, that is different; it is long and wide and at either end are vistas such as few other streets can offer. Indeed, the view of 'Scotland's Disgrace', the half-finished replica of the Athenian Parthenon which was meant to commemorate Waterloo, is typical of the accidental glories of this famous thoroughfare, glories that owe as much to nature as to man, for it is the overall scenic effect that makes Edinburgh what it is and which saves the flatter, uninspired parts of the New Town from mundanity. Edinburgh is still the most beautiful city for its size in Great Britain, despite modern depredations and the

Randolph Crescent Gardens, with Drumsheugh Toll and Corstophine Hill, Edinburgh. Described by the Corporation as "just a clump of trees", these gardens were the subject of a notable Public Enquiry in 1958, when the battle for the New Town was first joined.

foolish refusal of its authorities to apply logical planning-standards to its traffic, and in some cases cultural problems. The Festival City has no opera house, though Mr Heath when Prime Minister offered £2 million of government aid if the local authority would find the rest, and between the wars that most gifted and scholarly of artists, John Kinross, devised a monumental grouping in which a memorial to those who died in the First War would be expressed in an artistic and civic centre for the living.

After the last war Sir Patrick Abercrombie was employed at considerable expense to provide an overall plan for the city and produced a detailed and sensible one in which, amongst other things, the A1 would be sent below Princes Street, and thus through-traffic separated from local. It went unimplemented, and then another costly report was ordered from another expert and similarly ignored. Yet we carry on with a

A view of the Grassmarket in Edinburgh, with Heriot's Hospital in the background. Immediately below is the site of former public executions.

festival run 'on a shoe-string' and a commercial life in which the fiction is maintained that Edinburgh is not like other cities, not like Glasgow, for instance, which thrives on industry and is not supposed to be culturally minded, though in the past it certainly has been, perhaps more so than Edinburgh. (Glasgow cradled its very own school of art, which was neither 'national' nor burghal but international.) Oddly enough, Glaswegians themselves contribute to this Edinburgh fiction, coming to the capital in shoals on holidays to shop, especially at Marks & Spencers, which cannot possibly be better than at home. I have even heard a Glaswegian describe coming to Edinburgh as going into the country!

So Edinburgh is primarily a city of legends and of views, created as if by accident, an old historic town running down the ridge of a volcanic hill that stretches from the castle to Holyroodhouse, the Dunedin of the Picts and the Edwins-

Edinburgh and the distant Pentlands, with Daniel Stewart's College in the foreground. – the view from Fettes old playing-fields.

borough of the Northumbrians. There was a windy wilderness to the south and a marshy loch to the north until a newer town was built on the far side of the loch, which was drained to accommodate the railway, when Princes Street was created along the Lang Walk, the path that came in from the west and joined the road from Leith where the present Register House and General Post Office are. There is the famous view of the castle from Princes Street, but also a splendid one from the castle over the street to Leith, the Firth of Forth and Fife. There are also views of Edinburgh itself, seen from outside, a marvellous one coming from Glasgow via Corstorphine Road, and huge panoramas from the south, the Pentlands and above Dalkeith, with shorter, less extensive ones nearer at hand. The city from Fettes playing-fields, for example, makes one think of those nineteenth-century prints I men-

144

tioned, with Gothic-Revival turrets and towers that might almost suggest the Kremlin or a distant view of Prague rather than another boys' school.

New York and London often describe themselves as 'cities of villages', but perhaps only Edinburgh really is. One of the most authentic of Edinburgh villages is almost in the middle of it. I refer to the hamlet of Water of Leith which Robert Louis Stevenson described as "the Herculaneum of the North". I have a glimpse of it from my windows, below Telford's Dean Bridge, a remnant of another world that has survived because the new high-level bridge bypasses it. The original low-level one, over which everyone entering the city from Queensferry had to pass, was down there amongst the red-pantiled houses with their cobbled alleys and ancient Tolbooth. After a period of decay and depopulation, the Water of Leith, now somewhat misnamed as the 'Dean Village', which formerly stood high above the river near the Dean Cemetery, has become desirable as a small dormitory away from the noise and stour of the streets above – yet a bare stone's throw from them. About eighty years ago my great-uncle restored the old Tolbooth, originally the granary of the canons of Holyrood and then the headquarters of the Edinburgh baxters, or bakers, as a mission attached to St Mary's Cathedral, but its life in that capacity ended with the demise or removal of most of the congregation. Theirs was the only Christian community in the village; they had been baptized in the mission, been to the Sunday school, and been married by the cathedral clergy till there were no more to come. The few that remained were shifted from their antique but homely houses to cold, hygienic apartments on a housing-estate where they knew no one and quickly faded away. When a report was made to the city on the subject of the future of the Water of Leith, it laid particular stress on the importance of maintaining the unique quality of the place and the character of the people, but like other reports was largely ignored.

Stevenson's own village was Swanston, a place of long, low, thatched cottages in a fold of the Pentlands, not of tall,

Newly thatched cottages in Robert Louis Stevenson's village, Swanston, Midlothian.

red-pantiled houses such as those in the 'Northern Herculaneum' by the Water of Leith. The Swanston cottages were recently restored, the thatching having to be done with Norfolk
reeds by an eastern counties craftsman, there being no thatchers left in Scotland. The result is good, and the whitewash
with which the walls have been spruced up is fresh and attractive. One wonders, however, what RLS would have
thought of them. Scotland was not a very clean country in his
day – it is clean only in parts now, and it certainly was not as
clinical and Swedish-looking as some of the latest restorations would indicate. It was not even like the New Town, in
which he was brought up, with its regulated black doors and
white windows. In Georgian times doors and windows were
either oak and not painted, or pine and painted brown or
stained. Scotland is an old-fashioned country, and thus I can
remember this very feature myself, before everything went
black and white and over-sophisticated. In Charlotte Square
the centre house, formerly the town residence of the Marquis

of Bute, retains to this day its unpainted oak door and is the residence of the Secretary of State for Scotland, but its example seems not to have been noticed.

The franking-stamps on letters posted in Edinburgh used to bear the words "The Festival City by the Sea", with a line-drawing of a deer leaping across what looked like a Highland background. Undoubtedly someone was hoping to get their tourist cake and eat it. In fact, it was nearly true, for one can see the Highlands from the higher parts of the city, and one is never very far from the sea. It is not a nice bit of sea, not until East Lothian is reached, and even there not really warm enough for pleasant bathing, hence the 'acclimatized' swimming-pools. Power-stations tend also to inhibit the holiday atmosphere, not to mention the remnants of erst-while coal-mining turned sour. Inland the environs are more rewarding, though even there electricity-pylons spoil some of the longer views – in the Pentlands for instance, a range of hills which at a distance are not dissimilar in silhouette to the Malverns and which are equally volcanic in origin. Once, looking down on Drummond of Hawthornden's old house near Roslin, my host, Sir James Williams Drummond, remarked, "One might almost be in the Highlands here." I knew what he meant: the deep, wooded glen, "impervious to the sun's rays", as Scott remarked, the turreted mansion and the sycamore tree under which Ben Jonson and the poet Drummond sat after the former had trudged all the way up from London to congratulate him. Behind ran the line of the Pentlands with no sign of a coal-bing or pylon to mar the view. One seemed miles from the industrial scene, yet practically in the middle of it.

Lothian has always been open to invasion by both armies and ideas; it remained Pictish when north of the Forth the Scots were masters, and became Northumbrian before the Normans arrived. It bore the brunt of Edward Plantagenet's attack and later that of his descendants, especially Henry VIII, who sent the Earl of Hertford up north to ravage the Low-lands from Berwick to Dundee; it was then the Border abbeys

A view of Ford, Midlothian, with the seventeenth-century house of the Frasers of Lovat in the foreground.

were sacked. Cromwell occupied the area, and Prince Charlie won his greatest and only really important victory near Edinburgh, at Prestonpans. All this time, however, and continuing to the present, Lothian has been receptive to economic and cultural movements emanating from the south and the Continent of Europe, and thus most of the buildings and indeed much of the way of life are less ostentatiously Scotch, more akin to things elsewhere. One must not exaggerate, of course, but where an Aberdeenshire laird, for example, would build himself a tall, defensive tower as late as the seventeenth century, in Lothian his equivalent would essay to create a comfortable, non-defensive manor-house. Others, possibly with business in the capital, erected small country retreats for themselves, a particularly fine specimen being at Ford, near Pathhead, where the L-shaped house of the Frasers of Lovat strikes the eye attractively by its orange colourwash and gay ogee-roofed stair-turret. The orange hue is a peculiarity of this part of Scotland and may have been invented to complement the red stone of the district; it is made by the simple expedient of mixing copper with the limewash.

The valley at Ford is crossed by Telford's viaduct, an almost exact copy of the one seen from my window spanning the Water of Leith, while round about are more interesting houses, including an Adam castle, now a girls' school, and Preston Hall. This was built by a retired Indian nabob to the plans of an Aberdeen-born architect and has in its grounds a handsome Classical folly which, intended but never used as the burial-place for the nabob and his family, recently served as a temporary resting-place for Ensign Ewart, who wrested the Eagle Standard from the foe at Waterloo and who normally reposes on the Castle Esplanade in Edinburgh.

Dotted around the countryside are numerous smaller houses of note, such as Pilmuir, which has the distinction of two quite different façades, one quaint and playful, the other plainer and symmetrically disposed, while inside are some of the very first sash windows made in Scotland. In the orchard is a fine 'lectern' doocot, with lean-to roof, and set in a garden

The 'lectern' doocot at Pilmuir, East Lothian.

wall are two bee-boles, holes for straw bee-skeps, or hives, still surviving. At Cakemuir a more martial note is struck by the sentry's walk at roof-level, a reminder that, as one approaches the Borders, internecine strife died hard; but in the garden is some intriguing statuary, most of it representing figures from Scott's novels, such as Saladin and Mary, Queen of Scots, who with her lover Bothwell spent a night here during their elopement.

Nearer the coast the Setons held sway, the same who carried so much weight in Aberdeenshire and who became the effectual ancestors of the Seton-Gordons. The Earl of Dunfermline, whom we have met before as Lord Fyvie, enlarged Pinkie House in Musselburgh in imitation of the celebrated Jacobean and Tudor mansions he knew in England and also lived at Seton Palace, since replaced by an Adam castle. His kinsman the Earl of Winton created Winton House, perhaps the most remarkable Scottish interpretation of southern-based ideas of the early-seventeenth century. The mason was no less a person than William Wallace, Master Mason to the King, for whose homecoming in 1617 he re-

Left: Straw bee-skeps set in their holes in the garden wall at Pilmuir, East Lothian.

'Saladin', one of several characters from Scott's novels that decorate the grounds of Cake-muir Tower, Mid-lothian.

stored and modernized the palace block at Edinburgh Castle. Wallace's greatest triumph at Winton, and a work of near genius, are the chimney-stalks, which in England would probably have been cast in brick but which are here carved in stone in the most fantastic shapes and patterns. The tradition of such fantasies was actually an old one for the Scots, who, ever faithful to the intricacies of Romanesque as opposed to Gothic, never quite lost their sculptural prowess. Inside, Winton boasts the finest and most elaborate Renaissance plaster ceilings of the period, created in part by the same craftsmen who later went on to decorate Glamis and Craigie-var but also by more consummate artists, possibly Italians, when 'the King's Room' was provided with a Florentine frieze and ceiling composed of national and royal emblems for occupation by Charles I, who stayed either here or at Seton during his coronation visit to Edinburgh. It would be

William Wallace's fantastic chimney-stalks at Winton, East Lothian.

interesting to know if this ceiling was ever coloured, as its Italian counterparts were – possibly not, as the bills say nothing about it, but we do know that the pristine white fretwork ceilings at Holyrood, similarly rich in decor and form, were painted, and old photographs show them still partly so.

Along the coast, power-stations and coal-mining have replaced salt-panning, which used to be the foremost activity here as in parts of Fife and, indeed, engendered free fights between participants and disputes not unlike the inter-Union rivalries we suffer today. Prestonpans, scene of the Jacobite victory of 1745, retains the nucleus of a typical Jacobean and Carolean burgh, with well preserved mercat cross and two most interesting houses, both built as country residences by Edinburgh magnates, Magdalens, which was the home of a law lord, and Northfields, that of a burgess of Edinburgh whose civic motto appears over the garden door. Nearby is Preston Tower which was abandoned by its laird after an attempt to adapt it to seventeenth-century living by adding a Renaissance pent-house to its already great height. In the grounds is a double doocot, showing how important it was to possess such things, as a status symbol, since royal permission was required to erect one, and as a source of winter fodder.

Further on is North Berwick, Edinburgh's Brighton, if one can imagine such a comparison, and Haddington, the principal town of East Lothian. I used to think of it in much the same way as Elgin, where a similar amount has been preserved by way of buildings and character, the image of a genuine old Scottish market-town, with broad High Street, steepled Town House, ample shops and ancient kirk of cathedral proportions. St Mary's Haddington has recently been completely restored, the formerly unroofed portion being covered by the ingenious use of fibre-glass vaulting, while the town has become an over-spill for Glasgow, its High Street the subject of a Civic Trust face-lift.

Near Haddington is Gifford, one of the first Scottish villages, by which I mean a place deliberately created as such from nothing. An older hamlet was moved by the Marquis of Tweeddale to build his new Palladian mansion, when he vacated Yester Castle, seat of the Giffards, with soft 'G' and an 'a', and their de Haye successors. While workmen were busy on the roof of the new Yester House, still unfinished in the mid-eighteenth century though begun in the seventeenth, they threw slates down on stragglers fleeing from the Highlanders at Prestonpans. They could see where the fugitives were bound for, hiding-places in the Lammermuirs. These first Border hills sweep down to the sea in Berwickshire to create a dramatic entry into Scotland by the A1 and also by rail, an introduction that must appear to fulfil the dreams of all but the most fastidious of Scotophiles.

At the northern end of this stretch is the chilly seaside resort of Dunbar, where the main-line trains still stop on request and the main road takes a wide bend to avoid it. The Haddingtons live close by at Tyninghame and, despite the general bleakness and windiness of the area, have made their estate famous for its woods. As long ago as the early-eighteenth century, this was so, proving the truth of Scott's opinion that

The quaint red-stone tower of the Town House at Dunbar, showing Netherlandish influence.

Right: An older masonic tradition in the ruins of St Baldred's Chapel at Tyninghame, near Dunbar.

Scotland need not be dour and treeless, for all you had to do was stick a slip or shoot in the ground and it would grow. He certainly proved it at Abbotsford, as the Earl of Haddington has done here, the woods coming right down to the sea's edge. It is curious the dislike of trees on the part of some Scots. It was noticed by Lord Cockburn when he remarked that no excuse was needed to cut a tree down, only to retain it or plant another, and not long ago, when the Cockburn Association proposed to Edinburgh Corporation that they might plant some elms in Elm Row, which had none, their suggestion was turned down, even when they offered to provide the plants.

Tyninghame House is a good example of Scotch-Jacobean designed during the 'Battle-of-the-Styles' period by William Burn, who was equally at home in the severest Doric, he being architect of the Spartan façade of Edinburgh Academy. Here, in a garden overlooked by turrets and towers, oriel windows and high, whimpled roofs is St Baldred's Chapel, a superb remnant of Romanesque architecture not quite serving the purpose of a folly but certainly a feature amongst the pergolas, its soft red sandstone carved exuberantly and repeated in the mansion itself. St Baldred was one of those local missionaries whose whereabouts in life as in death was always a bit of a mystery, he tending to be in more than one place at once. But what of it? He existed in some shape or form and certainly helped to make Christians out of our Bernician ancestors. At the southern end of the region is Eyemouth, with its amusement arcade, popular alike with Tynesiders on holiday and Fife fishermen at weekends. Then one suddenly comes to Berwick-upon-Tweed and Northumberland.

Berwick is unique on several scores: its immaculate 'Italian'

walls, its three bridges and its Anglo-Scottish background. For most of its history it was Scots, until the second half of the fifteenth century when it was swapped for Roxburgh; and a hundred years later it became a 'Free City' with its own 'Liberties', neither Scots nor English. So it remained until modern times when in the recent alteration in regional boundaries it was given to Northumberland. Yet it has English and Scots kirks and banks and is the market-town for Borderers on both sides of the Tweed. It was also, until a few years ago, the headquarters of the King's Own Scottish Borderers Regiment, the handsome barracks of which were designed by Sir John Vanbrugh, playwright turned architect. These were the first barracks built as such in Great Britain and have now become a museum, while the KOSBIES have moved to Dumfries.

It was over a somewhat shaky medieval bridge that the first king of both England and Scotland made his processional progress into England in 1603, a circumstance which caused him to have it repaired and strengthened as we see it today. The higher road bridge was opened by Edward VIII, as Prince of Wales, and is of an entirely different kind, its northern abutment breaking the 'Italian' walls for the first time in their history. As for Stephenson's many-arched railway bridge, it came to an end near the site of Edward Plantagenet's castle, the place where he pronounced John de Baliol rightful heir to the Scottish throne – a perfectly correct decision, as it proved, but not a popular one. Edward's walls followed a much smaller circumference than the fifteenth-century ones and were not designed to resist artillery; when his castle was breached by the railway engineers in order to make Berwick Station, Robert Stephenson commented that it marked the final breaking-down of the divisions between the two countries. Berwick's 'Liberties' continue for a mile or two on both sides of the river, then one is back in Scotland, in Berwickshire, with its red sandstone, abbeys and pele-towers, splendid country estates, woods and farmlands, a county whose furrows have never been soiled by the invader since the 'Rough Wooing', when Henry VIII, unable to get Mary, Queen of Scots, as the spouse for his ailing son Edward by fair means, tried foul.

In a country with so many rivers and lochs, Scotland of course boasts a remarkable number of bridges, large and small, arched and suspended, magnificent and simple, and the three at Berwick, albeit shared with a neighbour, might be said to typify the different types. At Loan End, however, is a fine chain bridge, dating from the early-nineteenth century, and at Coldstream one of Smeaton's elegant Georgian bridges, in the mould of others at Banff and Perth. It was over an earlier Tweed bridge that Monk took the future Coldstream Guards, when he marched on London and proclaimed Charles II, while at Coldstream too is The Hirsel, seat of Lord

John Smeaton's bridge over the Tweed at Coldstream, Berwickshire.

Home. He was the last of the disinterested type of leader in which this country used to specialize, the type who put their country first, like good soldiers. Unfortunately he came too late to prove his worth as Prime Minister, though amply doing so at the Foreign Office.

The Borders produced St Cuthbert, who was a shepherd-boy from Melrose, and Scott, to name but two illustrious sons, and are visited as much for their ruined abbeys as anything else. Their woollen-mills, mainly along the Tweed, have become internationally known, and the word 'Tweed' has travelled via the Outer Isles round the world. St Cuthbert, who became a bishop and is buried in Durham Cathedral, has had a strange metamorphosis which non-Scots may find unfamiliar since it is only in Scotland that the Co-operative Society is named after him. Why this is so, I simply do not know. The abbeys were mostly Cistercian, but not all, and the monks found the best places for their settlements by rivers, under hills; they did much for the people, teaching them new methods of farming and the gentry how to read and write. Eventually, however, they got too rich and powerful, until the Edwards sacked their monasteries, then Richard II, and finally Henry VIII's henchman, Hertford, who appeared in two different coronets, an earl's to begin with and then a duke's, and as supporter of two different religions, Papist and Protestant. On the first occasion he headed the destroyers of Melrose under a banner bearing the effigy of the Mother of God, after whom the abbey was named. The Knox faction came afterwards for the pickings, when the townspeople of Kelso, who had fought alongside the monks against Hertford, attacked that abbey and drove the inmates out. Jedburgh was luckier: its frame survived – indeed still survives and could, with a little patience, be restored as a church. Dryburgh suffered very badly, not so much from the English as from its own lairds, who inherited the former spiritual lordships and took what they wanted by way of stone and fittings for their houses.

Dryburgh enjoyed a new notoriety as the burial-place of 'the Bard of Abbotsford', whose horse stopped, halting the funeral procession *en route* at what has become known as 'Scott's View', overlooking the Tweed and the Eildon hills.

The ruins of Dryburgh Abbey in their park-like setting. Scott and Earl Haig are buried here.

Smailholm Tower, a favourite haunt of the young Walter Scott, whose grandparents had a farm nearby.

Then it became celebrated once more as the burial-place of another famous Scotsman, Earl Haig of Bemersyde, whose Border tower stands not far away. All around is the park created by earlier post-Reformation landowners, especially by that Earl of Buchan who, with great theatricality but little sense of the appropriate, arranged the details of Sir Walter's funeral (prematurely as it turned out, since he himself died first) and did not hesitate to tell his victim the full details. The Earl erected in the grounds of Dryburgh two statues, one of James II of the Fiery Face, who lost his life in the siege of Roxburgh, the other of James I, who pacified the Borders and most of the rest of Scotland and from whom the Earl of Buchan was descended in the illegitimate line.

Scott was actually born and brought up in Edinburgh, in the Old Town, and like Henry Cockburn lived through the transition from that to the new, his house in North Castle Street being one of the first to show any demonstrable sophistication by way of a pediment and bow window. His grand-

A great Border house, Mellerstain – the work of a Baillie laird with assistance from William and Robert Adam.

parents lived on a farm at Smailholm, and it was surely on his boyhood visits to them that he acquired his love of the Border Country, especially since Smailholm Tower is perhaps one of the most evocative and romantically sited of any of the so-called peles. (They are not really peles – that name refers to the earlier wooden palisades that were not superseded by stone structures until the mid-fifteenth century.) Smailholm rises like some grim sentinel on a volcanic outcrop, above a lochan in the midst of the wildest and most desolate of moon-landscapes, giving no indication of the meadows and woods that cover so much of the surrounding district. The tower is not even particularly old, dating from as late as the end of the seventeenth century, and cannot, therefore, have been intended as a pele of any sort.

Not far away is another high-sited tower, Hume Castle, a folly with huge crenellations which, however, served as a watch-out during the Napoleonic Wars when a French invasion was feared. Below that, in the most sumptuous of parks, is Mellerstain, a Border seat of palace proportions, partly the work of William Adam, partly of its Baillie laird, who had been to Italy; partly also of Robert Adam, one of whose finest rooms, the library, is here. Mellerstain is castellated, but in a purely decorative manner, and the park has its thatched-cottage follies and other amusing features, plus a lake with a background vista of The Cheviot, already in England. It is not the only very grand house hereabouts: Floors, for instance, the Kelso seat of the Duke of Roxburghe, is larger and was begun by William Adam, working under the influence of Vanbrugh, while at Mertoun, on a particularly attractive bend of the Tweed, is the home of the Duke of Sutherland, a rare Borderland design by Sir William Bruce undertaken for a relative of his second wife, who was a Scot of Harden. The Duke of Buccleuch, who has a house at Bowhill, near Selkirk, is the largest landowner in Britain after the Forestry Commission and British Rail, and his chief seats are at Boughton, in Northamptonshire, and Drumlanrig Castle, in Dumfriesshire. Then there is Manderston, based on Kedleston and designed by the consummate John Kinross for Lady Miller, who was a Curzon and whose husband's horses won the Derby twice. Kinross not only created a chaste mansion in the style of Robert Adam but surrounded it with splendid gardens and outhouses, some of the latter in the Scots vernacular, notably a tea-house resembling a Border tower and a gardener's lodge reminiscent of Argyll's Lodging in Stirling.

The true Border counties, those actually bordering on England, are Berwickshire, Roxburghshire and Dumfriesshire, the latter now thrown in with Galloway and treated separately. Neither Selkirkshire nor Peeblesshire touches the border anywhere, though both are normally considered as being 'in the Borders'. This is perhaps because the Tweed and its tributaries run through them, and, of course, Scott was 'Shirra', or Sheriff, of Selkirk, a post he was loved for rather than the reverse. He liked dispensing a little rough justice, using his prerogative to fine folk lightly or even letting them off with a lairdly homily. Selkirkshire has the highest average altitude in the country and was the home of the 'Ettrick Shepherd', James Hogg, who adored Scott and whose affection was rewarded by a genuine regard on the part of the more famous man. Abbotsford is just round the corner, and despite the enormous amount of tourism that assails it, there is still an air about the place that is worth seeking out. One is surely also permitted not only to admire but to smile happily at all the curiosities displayed in Scott's old abode. He may have played at being the 'squire', a sort of Scots Roger de Coverley, but he carried it off superbly, so that 'Gala Days' at Abbotsford were missed by few and remembered with joy by all. The architecture of the house may defy the rules, yet, seen against much that came after it, it seems positively subdued by comparison, its vagaries twice as interesting.

Amongst Scott's harmless fables was the one about Montrose after Philiphaugh. When the defeated Royalist was persuaded to call on the Earl of Traquair and ask for shelter, the legend goes, he knocked on the door long and loud, but there was no answer – not, however, on the existing beautiful knocker, for it was not there in Montrose's day. Traquair got its last face-lift at the end of the seventeenth century, when the knocker was installed, and since then, except for an occasional paint-up, it has been untouched, its lairds advertising it as the oldest inhabited house in Scotland. It may have rivals for that position, but it must have been continuously lived in since the thirteenth century at least, which is pretty good. There are other romantic stories about the place, the best known concerning the 'Steekit yetts', or gates, which were supposed to have been closed since Prince Charlie passed through them in 1745, not to be re-opened until a Stuart should regain the throne. There is no proof that the Prince ever visited Traquair, and a more plausible theory is that they were closed after the funeral procession of the last Countess, when Jacobite families were not permitted the use of coaches and horses except for such lugubrious purposes. More likely still, these gates have never been opened, for they have no

The Bear Gates at Traquair – the famous "steekit yetts" may, in fact, have been built as a folly.

hinges. They are probably folly gates, built as a feature at the end of a grass avenue. But what a wonderful field of conjecture they provide, and what a success for those who created them!

One of the most celebrated and picturesque views in the Borders is of Neidpath Castle perched on its eminence above the Tweed to the west of Peebles. This vision epitomizes the whole atmosphere of the region, scenic, poetical and historic, all that Scott invoked in his writing and to which anyone with a heart must willingly and automatically respond. It does not, on the other hand, have such a romantic history as Traquair, though it may be just as old. It was a Norman redoubt, not a Border 'pele' in origin, and belonged to the Frasers of Lovat before they moved north to Aberdeenshire. Later it fell to the Hays of Yester and eventually came to the earls of Wemyss whose heirs bear but do not use the title of Lord Neidpath. The reason for this is that several so-named heirs have met tragic deaths: a Lord Neidpath suffered for his constancy to the Stuart cause in the eighteenth century, and even a modern Lord Neidpath died tragically, so there is no one now known as Lord Neidpath. Further west from here the Tweed waters the land of John Buchan, a country of grassy hills and woolly sheep where he was brought up, the son of a parish minister. A low pass takes one over into Dumfriesshire, via the Devil's Beeftub, a natural hide-out for reivers who herded stolen cattle there until it was safe to drive them into their own byres. Not far away is Eskdalemuir, the wettest and one of the coldest places in Scotland where meteorological records are kept.

The southern side of the Border hills around Moffat have been described as typifying 'Bonnie Scotland' on account of the warmer climate, abundance of foliage, blossoming orchards and prosperous farms, all in direct contrast to the balder northern slopes over which one passes to get there. The frightening Castle of Hermitage is in the uplands between, a castle of beastly murders and incredible cruelty, the place where Mary, Queen of Scots, nearly killed herself riding to meet Bothwell. At the bottom of the valley is the restored tower called Gilnockie but which is really Hollows, Gilnockie having been demolished some years ago to make room for a new footbridge over the Esk. Here again the railway company have shown imagination and a sense of history by perpetuating the name in the nearest station. Gilnockie was said to have been the redoubt of one Johnnie Armstrong, a sort of Border Robin Hood, if one can believe the myths told about him – which one cannot, since the truth is he was a gangster who robbed all and sundry, rich and poor, English and Scots, and killed when thwarted. Eventually James V arrived on the scene and had him hanged. Yet he has gone down to history, local history anyway, as a folk-hero, when he was nothing of the sort. Nor was he 'of Gilnockie', as is claimed. However, the present occupiers of Hollows Tower, with Armstrong blood in their veins, have restored it very nicely indeed and are to be congratulated on their work.

Looking into Lanarkshire, with Tinto in the distance. This view from the kirkyard at Skirling, Peeblesshire, is reminiscent of New Zealand with its grazing sheep and scattered farms.

CHAPTER FIVE

LANARK, GLASGOW AND THE WEST

PEEBLESSHIRE MERGES into Lanarkshire and crosses the watershed between Tweed and Clyde almost imperceptibly. It used to be marked by red roads, which made a change from the usual tarmacadam, but the county has recently given up its happy practice of laying red granite chippings on top and has gone all black like nearly everyone else – a pity, as the red helped to give Lanarkshire its rather special character. It is the county of Sir William Wallace and of Scott's 'Talisman', or Lee Penny, which is still kept by the Macdonalds of Lee, successors to the Lockharts of that Ilk, into whom they married. It was one of them, incidentally, whom the sculptor used as the model for the kilted Highlander that surmounts the memorial at the head of Glenfinnan, near where Prince Charlie raised his standard, so that the figure is actually a Lowlander. Wallace is associated with Lamington, where they are said to keep his chair and in whose kirk he was married, but not in the present 'God Box', surely – the one that Burns found so cold, as regards both its congregation and its minister, though it does keep a Romanesque door that the future Guardian of the Realm may have seen. He began his career of physical opposition to the English in Lanark, where there is an extraordinarily naïve statue of him, as unheroic and un-soldierly as could possibly be conceived, more like a podgy personage in a Wagner opera.

New Lanark has attracted a certain amount of interest since the war, being heralded as a rare survival of early Socialist experiment, the site of a workers' co-operative. The village, in the valley below Lanark proper, was founded towards the end of the eighteenth century by David Dale, a Glasgow capitalist, as a model cotton-manufacturing centre, and it was his son-in-law, Robert Owen, who as manager experimented with workers' participation schemes. They actually failed, and one suspects that the degree of patronage involved would not really suit our modern radicals, however much they may protest to the contrary at the safe distance of more than a century of Marxist propaganda. It is certainly strange how this sort of thing has suddenly come into prominence and indeed fashion. I recall, for instance, that when it was proposed to demolish George Square in Edinburgh, the architect for the University, the philistine in this case, was in favour of demolition, naturally, yet as soon as some danger cropped up in respect of New Lanark, that same person, a former President of the RIBA, rushed to the rescue and joined the newly formed preservation society. George Square was patrician, even bourgeois in taste, not plebeian and folksy like New Lanark, so was of no account and, to the shame of all concerned, was destroyed utterly except for one side which survived largely because the house in which Scott was brought up stood there. Robert Owen, by the way, lived at Braxfield, the erstwhile home of the law-lord of that name whose character was denigrated by Cockburn, undeservedly as it turned out, and which gave Robert Louis Stevenson the idea for his *Weir of Hermiston*, the story of the 'hanging judge' who at the end of the day found his own son before him on a charge of murder

Middle Clydesdale is dominated from all angles by the hill known as Tinto, whose well defined outline and central position put one in mind of Bennachie, in Aberdeenshire. It is already visible before one leaves Peeblesshire, rising as a slight cone in the near distance and filling in the background to the farming communities round about. It is not the only hill of consequence in the neighbourhood, however, for there is also Culter Fell, below which is the village of Culter, and the typical long, low, whitewashed laird's house which is the

Culter, a typical 'bonnet' laird's house in Clydesdale.

home of Victor Ferrier Noel Paton, Lord Ferrier, whose grandfather was none other than Sir Joseph Noel Paton, Limner to the Queen in Scotland and perhaps the most popular Scots Romantic painter of the nineteenth century. He was more than that, a considerable philosopher and student of religion, a connoisseur *sans pareil* of arms and armour. His sister was married to the pioneer photographer D. O. Hill, and some of the Noel Paton armour may be seen in his historic mock-ups. Interestingly enough, Sir Joseph discovered that amongst his duties as royal limner was that of attending the sovereign in person. Accordingly he wrote to Queen Victoria and announced his intention of coming to see her with his family. Possibly to his surprise, he was actually invited to Windsor as a result of this, and down south they all went, the children getting on famously with the Queen, once she had assured them she was not the wicked lady who cut off the head of Mary, Queen of Scots!

There are many legends about Tinto, the best known perhaps that which declares that no matter how ungainly or whatever colour a girl may be, take her up to the top of the

Tinto Hill, dominating the view in the Clyde Valley near Lamington, Lanarkshire.

hill, and the wind will blow her a man. The Clyde flows at the foot, or rather describes an arc around it on its way north to Glasgow and the industrial heart of the country. The scenery is unexpectedly attractive, green and welcoming, especially after Beattock and the bleak uplands further south, and just before Lanark everything comes together, at Hyndford Bridge, where communications between east and west, north and south, meet in force. The main road across Scotland, from Edinburgh to Ayr, crosses that from Carlisle to Glasgow here, leading over rolling countryside to Douglas and the west coast, arriving first at Castlemains, modest weekend retreat of Lord Home, since the demolition of Douglas Castle, which was too big and in danger of collapse from underground coal-workings. The castle was begun by the one and only Duke of Douglas who instructed the Adam brothers to make a replica, only much larger, of Inveraray Castle, seat of the Duke of Argyll. Only half, at the most, was

St Bride's Kirk, Douglas, burial-place of Scotland's most famous family.

ever completed, and nothing much of that remains except a store of ceremonial cannons which once graced the fake battlements, plus some fine heraldic glass which has been put into the tiny episcopal church of Sancta Sophia in Douglas.

Nearby is St Bride's, probably the most historic private chapel in Scotland, and one with a terrible early record. The present chapel dates from the fourteenth century and is a rebuilding of the one into which 'the Good Sir James', Bruce's paladin, drove the English garrison and killed them all, making a pile of the bodies and then burning them. His heart is said to be amongst those reposing in little heart-shaped receptacles in the chapel (the heart being the Douglas emblem), but this is doubtful. St Bride's is full of Douglas dust, ancient and modern, just the same, and has been glazed with medieval glass from Canterbury. The Douglases were the most powerful people in Scotland after the king and occasionally surpassed even him, hence the feud whereby a

The mausoleum of Alexander, tenth Duke of Hamilton, son-in-law of William Beckford of Fonthill.

Right: The ruins of Bothwell Castle, built by Guillaume de Moravia and dismantled by Bruce.

number of Douglases were assassinated at royal instigation. They married into the Stewarts, and one became Duke of Touraine, in France, and was buried in the cathedral at Orleans, with his brother, when both fell in battle under the banner of Joan of Arc.

It is remarkable how Douglas a district Clydeside is, and as one passes northwards, one meets site after site connected with either them or their Hamilton associates. At Tillietudlem (which is the fictitious name given to Craignethan by Scott, who was offered a home there before he decided to build Abbotsford) is the castle of a bastard in the line, a great mason but also a great rogue who was executed for treason, though not before masterminding James V's new hunting-lodge at Falkland. The valley hereabouts is white with blossom in spring; it is a land of orchards and market gardens such as no other part of Scotland and few in England rival in so concentrated a form. Further north, factories, mines and tower-blocks proliferate amidst transformation-scenes of all sorts; the ground itself has shifted and sunk, so that Hamilton

Palace was actually taken down stone by stone with the idea of re-erecting it across the Atlantic. The domed mausoleum built by Beckford of Fonthill's son-in-law when he became Duke of Hamilton was also to have gone, but it still stands, when the rest of the scheme was found impossible. Based on Hadrian's tomb in Rome, it used to enshrine the ancient Egyptian sarcophagus in which the Duke, definitely suffering from *folie de grandeur*, once reposed, but he has since been taken to a public cemetery, while the mausoleum itself sinks slowly into the black sludge against a background of sky-scrapers and smoke.

This weird reminder of the ephemeralness of man is not exhausted here, for at Chatelherault, the Baroque stables, or 'Dogges Kennel', designed by William Adam, survive on the edge of a sand-pit, poised between preservation and imminent destruction. No one knows what to do with this remarkable structure: it cannot be used where it is, nor is it permitted to remove it. There is a certain amount of greenery round-about and in one such oasis stands Bothwell Castle which, like Tillietudlem, was given by Lord Home's father to the nation and is now in the care of Ancient Monuments. It was the creation of William de Moravia, of the same family as the first bishop of Caithness and founders of the county of Moray, and boasted a magnificent round 'keep' until half was dismantled by Bruce after Edward Plantagenet's defeat. It should definitely be seen, both for its wooded site beside the river and for itself, as an example of a different kind of change and decay, proof of how much better they built in the thirteenth century than in later ages.

Beyond Bothwell one is in the suburbs of Glasgow, once described as 'the second city of the Empire' and now one of the largest Victorian cities in Britain. It may have been *the* largest until someone decided to 'do a Los Angeles' in the middle of it – that is, to remove the heart and run a high-level motorway right through, crossing the Clyde at roof-level and thus removing all sense of being in Glasgow at all. Of course it was a good scheme to bypass the centre, but that is not what they have done; instead a vital part has been levelled to the ground and filled with a maze of traffic. The mistake has not so far been imitated elsewhere in Scotland, at least not on such a devastating scale, and the Glasgow example may have succeeded in drawing people's attention to other dangers and stopping further destruction before it was too late. This must surely apply to the recent controversy over the façades along Great Western Road, which now looks marvellous, the 'Greek Thomson' fronts all cleaned up and work proceeding on less chaste neighbours. Indeed, when the Grosvenor Hotel was damaged by fire, and the proprietors proposed rebuilding in another idiom, the uproar was such that this particular façade, which is part of a continuous pattern of neo-Baroque arches, columns and balconies, is going back exactly as before, only with synthetic materials being used to simulate the old stonework.

To become the largest Victorian city in Britain (almost a sort of small Paris on the Haussmann model, all parallel streets and regular façades with, here and there, examples of that over-blown Baroque which had its apotheosis in Garnier's Opera), Glasgow had to destroy what earlier travellers had described as the most beautiful little city in Scotland, a green and pleasant place with houses and churches lining the sylvan Clyde like those of Oxford or Cambridge. There was a bishop's castle, demolished to make room for Robert Adam's Royal Infirmary, itself replaced since by a bigger, more vulgar building, and a splendid Renaissance university which went almost without a trace, to be rebuilt on a different site by Sir George Gilbert Scott – and that too has since been spoilt by uncomplementary modern additions. The Cross, where the bells ring out the old and in the new, was designed by the late Mrs Edith Hughes, a woman architect of my acquaintance, as a replica of the original. And that is about all there is to say about old Glasgow and the beautiful little city by the Clyde, but for the cathedral, whose survival, if not quite a miracle, is certainly remarkable. Opposite is a lonely Provand's Lordship, where the canons used to live. It is now a squirrel's museum, by which I mean it is chock-a-block with historical objects, from furniture to fire-irons, including a portrait of Mary, Queen of Scots, who is reputed to have stayed there.

St Mungo's Cathedral, the largest and finest medieval church in Scotland and the only pre-Reformation cathedral on the mainland to escape destruction in the sixteenth century, was saved by the intervention of the townspeople themselves, who prevented Knox's orders being carried out. In the Victorianization of the city, it was again placed in danger by both iconoclasts and improvers, when the two western towers were removed because they were asymmetrical and of different heights, like Chartres! Papal bulls and other documents that were housed in one of them were scattered in the street and burned as rubbish during this exercise, some pieces being saved by passers-by. Happily no worse befell the cathedral except for the insertion of German painted glass, in place of plain, now mostly removed, and the setting-up of a huge statue of Knox on the highest point of Glasgow

*The view of St Mungo's Cathedral, Glasgow, from the necropolis, with
the Royal Infirmary hemming it in, right.*

necropolis which overlooks St Mungo's. One would never
think that the burn that flows between was the scene of a
miracle performed by Glasgow's saint and that the holy
man's tomb in the crypt was a great place of pilgrimage in the
Middle Ages, the inspiration no doubt of the city's motto,
"Let Glasgow flourish, by the preaching of the Word", of
which only the first half is usually remembered.

Glasgow has flourished, however, and unlike Edinburgh,
where culture is officially established in the Arts Council
Premises and in the National Collections, it is a city which
has made its own art and gained from the connoisseurship
and generosity of its citizens. One need only mention Sir
William Burrell in this connection, for he left one of the
largest and finest collections of paintings and *objets d'art* in
European history to Glasgow, plus funds for its housing and
maintenance. That was a generation ago, and only now, after
many vicissitudes and much procrastination, is a suitable

The weir and mill on the River Cart in the grounds of Pollok House, Glasgow.

gallery in preparation, in the grounds of Pollok House. More positively, and before this, the Glasgow School arose, as both a movement and a building, the latter designed by the celebrated Charles Rennie Mackintosh, a key figure in the history of Art Nouveau. The Scottish Colourists, and 'the Glasgow Boys', as they were called, were something else. They were much influenced by the French Impressionists and later the Fauvists but added their own dimensions. They studied in Paris and tended to spend their holidays abroad, which makes it no surprise, perhaps, that the Glasgow Art Gallery contains so many Impressionist paintings, but that gallery is also full of other gifts from connoisseur citizens in the form of sculpture, furniture, textiles, porcelain, glass and especially arms and armour. Where Edinburgh may score over Glasgow is in contemporary art, but then that is now much more a matter of fashion than of deep-rooted taste; its roots are not really here, nor is it often the subject of popular appreciation.

Pollok House, in whose grounds the Burrell Collection will in due course be displayed and kept, was designed by William Adam and completed after his death. It is plain and proper and very Scotch and was the home of the Stirling Maxwells, a family of Saxon origin who came up from Dumfriesshire long ago and whose cultural record is second to none. Sir John Stirling Maxwell's father collected Spanish art in particular, and his and his son's furniture and *objets d'art* now stand in the rooms more or less as they were left. The park around was laid out with gazebos and other delights by Sir John, partly with the help of Sir Rowand Anderson, an architect whose approach was more practical than many then or now – he actually saved his clients money! In front of the house runs the River Cart, and over it crosses Adam's handsome Palladian bridge, with a view towards an old mill that seems so far removed from the normal life of the city as to be almost fanciful. Yet it is a working mill, and river and wooded banks do run through an otherwise entirely urbanized environment.

Sir John Stirling Maxwell's interests ran to other things besides gardens and works of art, for he was a pioneer preservationist whose love of Scottish history and architecture caused him to write his *Shrines and Homes of Scotland*, in which he tried to point out the dangers of demolition and maladaptation in his native land, illustrating his case with numerous pictures. I like to think that my *Scotland's Historic Buildings* is in the same tradition; at least one critic said it was, which is heartening. It is also heartening that, despite the enormous amount of destruction that has taken place since *Shrines and Homes* first appeared, we still do have quite a lot left, and most of it now much safer than before, if not always properly looked after. Sir John was a founder member of the National Trust for Scotland and a Royal Commissioner for Ancient Monuments, the first building he saved for posterity being Crookston Castle, which was on his own estate and which he presented to the nation. The stone 'keep' was the seat of the Stewarts of Darnley and remained in their possession right

Crookston, a former redoubt of the Stewarts of Darnley, between Glasgow and Paisley. It was the first ancient building presented to the nation – by the late Sir John Stirling Maxwell Bart, of Pollok.

down to the time of Louise de Kéroualle, mistress of Charles II, to whom it had come, he being the great-grandson of long-legged Darnley himself – an odd metamorphosis, but of course the lady never lived there. Crookston stands on the summit of a motte, or artificial mound, and replaced a more ancient pele, or wooden palissade, itself protected by both a deep ditch and an outer ring of prickly hawthorns, which survive.

The surroundings of Glasgow are amongst the most attractive and varied in Europe, something like Milan's, with the Italian lakes, but also with the Riviera thrown in for good measure. The Highlands are almost on everyone's doorstep, Dumbarton and Loch Lomond practically in the suburbs, while the sea and lochs are no more than an hour's drive away. Glasgow has pleasant suburbs as such, more English perhaps than Edinburgh, more genuinely bourgeois. I have never understood why the terms 'bourgeois' and 'middle-class' should have acquired their present rather sneering connotation in some quarters. Without a middle class a country cannot really prosper, and most two-class societies, rulers and ruled, wish they had a buffer of some sort in the middle. The term 'bourgeois' properly refers to people living in a town, and it became a mild form of amusement amongst the so-called 'upper classes' when 'trade' started to take precedence over rank in the power-game, hence 'Lady Bracknell's' remarks anent folk rising "from the purple of industry". In France the middle class rules, and its superlative *cuisine* is enjoyed by all, hence the term 'bourgeois' has quite a different meaning there. Glasgow is a bourgeois city – so is Edinburgh if it comes to that, but the Edinburgh bourgeoisie is stiffer, more Swiss by comparison with Glasgow – 'East Windy, West Endy', as the saying goes. Glasgow's middle class, on the other hand, is extrovert and fun; its women used to be over-hatted in the days when they wore them; its men play, eat and drink more enthusiastically than their east-coast equivalents, and also make more money. The best time and place to appreciate the friendly open-heartedness of the Glaswegian is at a wedding in the west. It will reveal much of the secret of how to enjoy life without descending to coarseness or apologizing for one's pleasure.

There are other divergencies between the west and the east which are not always understood: the religious mix is not the same; then there is the Irish question, both northern and southern living together in the same region. There are many more Roman Catholics concentrated in Glasgow and environs than anywhere else in the country, and perhaps commensurate with this the Protestants stand out more sharply, their 'God Boxes' more appropriately named. The idea of a House of God was taken fairly literally in Georgian and early Victorian times, the kirk consisting of a simple rectangle, with the same sort of windows and doors as a house, even furniture in some cases, the main addition being a tower or bell-

*A characteristic eighteenth-century
'House Kirk' near Greenbank on
the outskirts of Glasgow.*

*Above right: Cloch Lighthouse on the Firth of Clyde, built by the Little
Cumbrae Lighthouse Trust in 1797. Note the fog-horn left.*

cot; and when one comes to think of it, there is no reason why
this should not be so. After all, Gothic buildings were much
the same to look at whether they were for secular or ecclesiastical use, except for their towers. Anyway, one can still find
some good Georgian and early Victorian kirks in the west,
while in Edinburgh the mock-Gothic fashion, with Low
Church Anglican undertones, has long since been the vogue
amongst many Presbyterians.

Dumbarton, despite its industrial outlook, marks the
ending of the Lowlands and the beginning of the Highlands,
but across the Clyde is Greenock, firmly Lowland yet
viewing Bute and Arran and much of Argyll against a
horizon of sea and hills that appears almost limitless. Then
there is Cloch Point with its famous lighthouse standing
beside the coast road, looking for all the world like an ordinary house, with crowsteps in the Scots vernacular, except
for its striped tower and projecting fog-horn. Further down,
at Largs, Great Cumbrae comes close to the shore, seeming

not an island but part of the bay, and on it, at Millport, is the tiny Cathedral of the Isles. This is probably the masterpiece of William Butterfield, architect of the Oxford Tractarians and better known for the red brick chapel of Keble College, Oxford, which houses Holman Hunt's 'Light of the World'. Here at Millport the polychrome tiles and coloured marbles so beloved of the Victorians have been used sparingly, the site perhaps inspiring less eclectic forms; and of course the cathedral, which only seats just over a hundred and is the smallest in the United Kingdom, is built of local stone and roofed with Ballachulish slates. With the provost's house and its adjuncts, the group is a rare gem which awaits a new lease of life in a world that has largely bypassed it, but for holiday-makers in the summer, when a fun-fair neighbours it.

All the way south is a string of resorts big and small, with the hills falling down to the sea as far as Saltcoats, where a

The whitewashed steadings of an Ayrshire farm viewed from an archway of Crossraguel Abbey.

great sandy bay opens, with Ayr at its centre. Ayrshire is a sort of Scottish Devon, only less accidental in its contours, where lush green fields are full of black-and-white cows munching contentedly, where cheese is made and labelled 'Scottish Cheddar' and where golf is played. It is the land of Robert Burns, though his family came from the north-east, where the name is spelled Burnes and pronounced in two syllables, as Fettes and Forbes and Foulis should be. The Burns cult is perhaps the most curiously illogical one in Scotland, for so many of the folk and ideas it represents are the very opposite to those he would have subscribed to. It has always been the aim of lesser mortals to add to their own meagre stature by trying to bring down to their level those who have done better than themselves or are actually better. "I kent his faither" is a typical Scottish comment on someone who has been successful in a way the speaker has not but wishes he had. So it is with Burns. He was a genius and displayed a sensitivity rare amongst his Ayrshire contemporaries. He was not a peasant, and he had no patience whatsoever with anyone or anything that was not straightforward and genuine. Yet it is ministers and other drol commentators who today pay such loud lip-service to him, often without fully understanding his works, taking bits out of context and making the exercise rather more self-congratulatory than a sincere tribute to the poet.

Ayr is a large and popular seaside resort, with a good beach, a race-course and golf at Troon. Unfortunately it has few particularly interesting buildings, a bridge and the tower of a fortified kirk in what was one more of Cromwell's citadels. Dismantled at the Restoration, the Roundhead fort was converted into a model factory and workers' housing-estate by Sir William Bruce, acting at the behest of an 'improving' earl of Eglinton. These earls were especially public-spirited, and at Eaglesham, nearer Glasgow, is an entire village erected by a late-Georgian scion of the same noble family, with delightful houses facing each other across a wide, sloping green, the burn that drove the mills flowing between. It was yet another earl of Eglinton who organized the famous Tournament in 1839, in the grounds of his Ayrshire seat, now demolished but for its 'Gothycke' gates. Eglinton Castle was designed by John Paterson, master of works at Culzean under Robert Adam. The Tournament typified the romantic age which Scott had done so much to foster and which produced such extraordinary and opposing characters as Victor Hugo and Louis Napoleon. The latter took part in the Tourney, bringing with him as esquire Fialin de Persigny, whom he afterwards made a duke, when, as Napoleon III, he consummated the whole romantic dream. Pierrefonds was restored, and Carcassonne and Paris were rebuilt, surely part of the same dream, though not, perhaps, directly resulting from participation in the Eglinton Tournament or studying the writings of Sir Walter Scott. In any case it rained most of the time, and the armour got rusty, while the would-be

The old mansion of Auchinleck, seat of James Boswell's father and the place where the biographer of Dr Johnson was brought up.

medievalists had to shelter under unchivalric umbrellas. The ball at night must have been amusing though, with all those tights and whimples, and it was very aristocratic and respectable; Queen Victoria would have approved, had she and Albert been there.

Quite near Eglinton rises the gaunt gable of what remains of Kilwinning Abbey, once one of the finest in Scotland and one of the few not royally founded. The Stewarts inhabited this part of the country in the days when they were still Hereditary Stewards and not yet kings, and they founded the great abbey of Paisley. They also erected Dundonald Castle on its isolated mount, presumably imitating their ancestral 'keep' at Dol, in Brittany, similarly sited by the sea and with a view for miles around. Samuel Johnson was taken to Dundonald by Boswell and made jokes about 'King Bob'. They made an excursion from Auchinleck, or 'Affleck' as it is pronounced, where the Doctor's Scottish friend was brought up

Ardrossan from Castle Hill. The ferries for Arran and the Isle of Man run from here, and the castle was that of the Montgomeries of Eglinton.

and his law-lord father was laird. It is a fine mansion, not, I think, designed by a member of the Adam family though copied from William Adam's design for Elie House, in Fife. In the grounds is the Boswell Mausoleum, which with Auchinleck is the property of a Boswell Trust, but so far no permanent use for the house has been found. The area is pitted with coal-mines, and other works, some of which may date from the lifetime of him whose fame does not equal that of Burns in his native land, his art being perhaps less obviously concerned with the 'brotherhood of man'.

Ardrossan, which overlooks Saltcoats and much of Ayrshire, coastal and inland, is a surprising place. From its castle hill one sees in the foreground refineries and chemical-works, set against that most inspiring of natural backgrounds which extends from here to Greenock and beyond, while to the south is the wide sweep of the Bay of Ayr, with the hills around Culzean and Ailsa Craig in the middle distance. 'Paddy's Milestone', as the latter is called, is composed of the right sort of granite for making curling-stones and has similarities with Staffa and the 'Giant's Causeway'. Ardrossan is where the ferries ply to the Isle of Man and Arran, but it also boasts some attractive early-Victorian houses, villas really, now mostly boarding-houses. I had never thought of staying there, and one suspects that those who do so, every year at about the same time, thrive on solid breakfasts and enormous high teas. Saltcoats is more modern, almost gay, while Irvine, which is not absolutely on the sea but has a wide river flowing through it, might almost be called sophisticated by comparison, that is if it had not already been nicknamed 'The Holy City' on account of its numerous tall church-towers. Inland are Kilmarnock and Kilmaurs, with a lovely little Town House, Rowallan Castle and the Covenanting villages of Fenwick – villages because there are upper and lower Fenwicks which were never on speaking-terms. Fenwick kirk is a cruciform one of elegant design, retaining external stairs to the galleries and on the pulpit an hour-glass. In the kirkyard are the graves of 'the martyrs', men whose fate was sealed by their own intransigence and refusal to acknowledge any form of human order and whose very obtuseness made them into martyrs. The rhyming lines on their gravestones are a mixture of arrogance and self-pity which is typical of professional malcontents, and one cannot help thinking that the little metal martyrs' crowns that appear above them were deserved. They were not kind people; they went into battle with ropes with which to hang their enemies, singing psalms as if they were the chosen people, their pistols at the ready.

Miners' villages proliferate in inland Ayrshire, one with the fascinating name of Patna. It is the only fascinating thing about it, and makes one think of curry and rice. It leads, however, via the valley of the Doon, into the Galloway hills and to Loch Doon. Here the river has been cleverly diverted by a tunnel under its natural watershed so that it can be sent into the upper Dee and thus top up the barrages going down to Kirkcudbright and the Solway Firth. An elaborate system has been devised, changing the valley into a series of lochs, the largest of which, Loch Ken, swells the Ken and produces scenery of Highland grandeur. Loch Doon itself is also now much bigger; its ancient castle, formerly standing on an island in the middle, was taken down stone by stone and rebuilt on a new site when the level of the water was raised. Would one still call it authentic, I wonder. Lochinvar Castle, on the other hand, was submerged when the waters of that loch were raised – a pity; if only for sentimental reasons, one would have liked to have seen it. It was the *caput*, or seat, of the Gordons of that Ilk, true Gordons who stayed in Galloway and made their names there. One was the last Archbishop of Glasgow and Galloway before the Reformation, taking advantage of that movement to marry, while another was the last of the Protestant archbishops, staying on some time after the Presbyterian Church was established in 1695. These Gordons were noted for their loyalty to the native line of kings; one entertained Mary, Queen of Scots, in adversity, and another was made Earl of Kenmore by a beleaguered Charles I. His successor was beheaded on Tower Hill with Lord Derwentwater after the failure of the 'Fifteen', both being allowed to arrive by coach, attended by their valets, and absolved from the ignominy of being drawn and quartered – this probably because the Earl of Derwentwater was a grandson of Charles II, his grandmother being Moll Davis, the actress.

One can reach Galloway through the Loch Doon gap or round the coast. I prefer the former, but the coast is more dramatic and takes one directly to Loch Ryan and Stranraer, the port for Larne and now very busy indeed with shuttle-services to and from Ulster. *En route* one passes Culzean and Dunure, both Kennedy places. Culzean is well known as one of the most exciting National Trust properties in the country, the most celebrated of Robert Adam's Scottish castles. It is now enhanced by a 'country park' which embraces much of the adjoining coastline, where the climate is so mild that trees

A sub-tropical garden set against the background of Robert Adam's mock-Gothic pavilions at Culzean.

grow down to the shore and in the gardens citrus fruits ripen. Alexander Nasmyth, a friend of Burns and an artist as well as amateur gardener, helped to lay out the park and afterwards painted a bird's eye view of the result from the sea. His employer, and the employer of Robert Adam, was civilized to a degree and knew almost as much about architecture as his architect. The Kennedys were a mixed bunch: one argued the night long with John Knox and seems to have got the better of him, while his successor, in order to obtain the abbatial lands of Crossraguel, roasted the last abbot alive till he got his signature to the transfer. This occurred at Dunure, where the castle is a ruin, but alongside is a well preserved specimen of a bee-hive doocot. It is right above the sea and most impressive. The Marquis of Ailsa, who is the head of the Kennedy family, has his estate office in Maybole, in the building where his ancestor argued with Knox and which is recognizable by

Above left: A fine example of a bee-hive doocot at Dunure. Above right: The tombstone of the children of William Lukup, "Mr of Works in Drumlanrig 1685", in Durisdeer churchyard.

its splendid oriel window on the top floor overlooking the main street.

The main road and railway route from Glasgow to Galloway actually pierces the Lowland hills to the east of the Loch Doon gap, going via Sanquhar through to the valley of the Nith and Dumfriesshire. Sanquhar was a seat of the earls of Queensberry, a branch of the Douglases, and in particular of that earl, later duke, who began the rebuilding on ambitious scale of Drumlanrig Castle, near Thornhill, in the reign of Charles I. The plan of the new castle, the last to be built as such, was based on Heriot's Hospital in Edinburgh, but the Civil War halted operations until the Restoration, when Sir William Bruce was consulted. Although the royal architect did not himself supervise the work, craftsmen engaged by him on his own house at Kinross went down to Dumfriesshire to make wrought-iron balustrades and add other specialist touches. The building was not completed till the reign of the last Stuart king, James VII and II, with James Smith, Bruce's successor as Surveyor to the Crown, in

The Lowther Hills viewed from the monumental entrance to Drumlanrig Castle, Dumfriesshire.

charge, the actual master of works being William Lukup, the grave of whose children may be seen in the churchyard at Durisdeer, not far from the castle, with an inscription mentioning him as mason at Drumlanrig.

Durisdeer kirk is well off the main road and little visited by those coming south to this pleasant land, not even by the 'doon haimers' themselves, as returning Dumfriesshire natives call themselves. Yet within the Queensberry Aisle is van Nost's black-and-white marble tomb to the second Duke and his spouse, a kinswoman of that Lord Burlington who was such a strong advocate of the Palladian style and who built Chiswick Villa. To me, notwithstanding the curvacious subtleties of the sculpture, the most extraordinary thing about this extravagant memorial is the way in which every piece of metal has been removed, in the case of rings by breaking the white marble fingers, on the assumption, surely wrong, that they were valuable!

Dumfriesshire was once called 'the Debatable Land' and was 'policed', though not always either efficiently or fairly, by a joint English and Scottish body with alternatively appointed leaders. It is dotted with towers, such as Elshieshields, which retains its large fire-bucket chimney used as a beacon in time of raids; Amisfield, which is the most perfect Scots tower of defence south of Aberdeenshire and stands roofed and immaculate in the garden of a Georgian mansion; and Spedlins, which is perhaps the most sinister ruin of its size and kind in the country. It is to be restored.

Anna Laurie came from Maxwelton, a much happier house based on an ancient tower, but now larger and most lavishly restored. She married a Ferguson of Craigdarroch, the pink and grey confection of whose charming William Adam house so nicely complements the surrounding Galloway landscape. Robert Burns had a farm nearby, at Ellisland, down by the Nith. It was whilst living there that he compèred and recorded the drinking-contest between three local lairds, Robert Riddel of Glenriddel, Sir Robert Laurie of Maxwelton and Alexander Ferguson of Craigdarroch, Anna Laurie's son. In 'The Whistle' the poet mentions "a little ivory whistle which ... whoever was the last able to blow it was entitled to carry off". The victor was Ferguson of Craigdarroch, and the whistle is still in the house.

The Fergusons, despite their Highland-sounding name, have been in Dumfriesshire since the fourteenth century at least, when Robert Bruce rewarded one of them for saving his life from drowning in the Nith with the gift of lands, since known as 'the Isle'. Isle Tower stands in the grounds of a more modern house to which it is attached and from which it can be entered. It is of considerable antiquity and not a Border tower in the same manner as most in the Debatable Land. The Bruces, of course, held their first Scottish feus in Annandale, while maintaining their Yorkshire estates around Guisborough, thus managing to face both ways. Later they married into the Gallovidian earls of Carrick and acquired property in Ayrshire, handing down the Carrick earldom to their descendants, including the present Prince of Wales, Duke of Rothesay. It all began in Dumfriesshire, however –

A pastoral scene with cattle and bridge in Nithsdale, near Thornhill, Dumfriesshire.

indeed, it was in the Kirk of the Greyfriars in Dumfries that Bruce murdered his adversary the Red Comyn, an act that haunted him ever afterwards and contributed to his desire to expiate the crime by having his heart taken to the Holy Land. He seems never to have come into violent contact with his principal rival for kingship, John de Baliol, whose father was the husband of the Lady Devorguilla, Princess of Galloway, and the endower of the Oxford college named after him. Devorguilla built the first bridge over the Nith at Dumfries, but it was probably of timber, and the existing many-arched stone one dates from the fifteenth century. She also carried her dead spouse's heart around with her in a little locket and finally caused it to be buried with her in the abbey of Douce Cœur which she founded near the Solway.

Sweetheart Abbey, to give it its English name, was not the oldest of the monastic establishments in Galloway, though through its romantic history it has become the best known. It features in Scott's novel *The Abbot*, in which the career of

Gilbert Broun, the last incumbent, is dramatized. Broun, protected by the laird, a Maxwell of Terreagles, steadfastly refused to budge when the Reformers came from Edinburgh to drive him away. He was supported by the people round about, many of whom had been taught by him as children, and he managed to survive for many years after the new regime had enforced its will elsewhere. Douce Cœur was Cistercian, allied to Melrose, as too was its Gallovidian sister, Dundrennan, near Kirkcudbright. Mary, Queen of Scots, went to Dundrennan after a night at Terreagles and sailed from the abbey slipway across the Solway to Cumberland

and exile. The ruins of Dundrennan, though scanty, are of a high order and possess certain similarities with Dryburgh, perhaps because they are mostly of the same period. Lord Cockburn saved them from continuous carting-away by farmers in the neighbourhood, who made dykes and out-buildings with the stones.

The local people similarly disposed of Glen Luce, further west, beginning the process in the mid-seventeenth century, the buildings standing empty but hale for nearly a century after the Reformation. The last abbot was a Hay, who had himself appointed to Glen Luce in good time to hand the property over to his descendants, one of whom built Park Hay, a tall L-shaped tower which has recently been 'done up' by the Department of the Environment. 'Done up' is the only fit description, since the building, undamaged and only slightly decayed, only needed renovating. It had rather at-tractive side pavilions which gave it poise and stability, but these were ruthlessly destroyed by the Ministry, while the rest of the masonry, after being carefully and expertly grouted and pointed, was covered over with the coating of masonic 'porridge', including crowsteps, chimney-copes, door- and window-surrounds, the lot. One would like to know on whose authority this was done and how an official body can demolish two perfectly good wings when ordinary mortals can scarcely do anything without permission.

Lincluden is not an abbey but a college, that is to say a colle-giate foundation with a provost, canons and choirboys and a church in which to function. In its present form it was the cre-ation of Archibald, Earl of Douglas, 'The Grim', who dis-possessed the nuns who held the property before because they were not sufficiently pliable to his wishes. In the ruins of the church is the flamboyant Gothic tomb of Margaret, Duchess of Touraine, and in the grounds is a Holy Mount or sanctuary around which the nuns planted a garden and placed small shrines. The original layout was discovered by the late Dr Douglas Simpson. 'Archibald the Grim' was illegitimate, but that did not stop him inheriting the Douglas patrimony, and

Threave, Galloway, stronghold of the Douglases until it was dismantled by James II 'of the Fiery Face'. It stands on an islet in the River Dee on the borders of Dumfries and Kirkcudbright.

it was he who held Threave Castle, on an island in the Dee between Castle Douglas and Kirkcudbright. The site is grim, like him, with the dark shadow of the vacant 'keep' standing up starkly against the sky and distant Galloway Hills, set on its flat little reedy islet off the banks of the river. It used "never to be without its tassle", a reference to the heads that habitually hung from its battlements. Subsequently the Douglases were dispossessed themselves, when James II of the Fiery Face arrived with one of his new-fangled cannon and dislodged them.

Kirkcudbright, like the Galloway landscape itself, held a special place in the affections of the Glasgow painters of last century and indeed is still beloved of artists and seekers after the picturesque in quiet and pleasant surroundings. E. A. Hornel, who was Australian born but of a Scottish origin, made his home here in Broughton House, which he left to the

The Dee at Kirkcudbright. Notwithstanding its sludgy harbour, the burgh is full of charm and was favoured by artists of the Glasgow School.

burgh and which is now a museum of his life and work, and furnished. He was a friend of George Henry, whose 'Galloway Landscape' set the style, the tone and the fame of this part of the world in artistic terms. He and Hornel were much attracted to the Orient, and Hornel's paintings often seem more like embroidery than normal canvas. In more modern times Kirkcudbright was the chosen residence of Charles Oppenheimer, a painter who paid no lip-service or anything else to current vogues but went on depicting what he saw as he saw it; his misty blue townscapes, with pinkish warmth showing through, remind one more of Stanley Cursiter, Queen's Limner for Scotland, whose paintings of Kirkwall seem not far removed in spirit from those of Kirkcudbright by Oppenheimer.

When visiting Kirkcudbright, I used to stay at the 'Selkirk Arms', kept by Sir Basil Douglas Hope Dunbar, who was a

197

The Galloway landscape – but without its black-and-white beltie cows. It was this broken-up, 'Celtic' scenery that appealed to painters of the late-nineteenth century and inspired the masterpiece in the genre by George Henry.

claimant to the earldom of Selkirk and a local laird, whence the inn's nomenclature. The Dunbars have been in Galloway since Norman times, and at Mochrum, in that wild region of scrub and marsh behind Wigtown and Newton Stewart, they had their fortalice. The Place of Mochrum, more of a fortified manor than a castle, was thoroughly restored earlier this century for the Butes, whose activities in this field were legion and exemplary. Staying at the 'Selkirk Arms' was like being in a country house for the weekend, with fine antique furniture, lovely oriental rugs, imaginative food and a generally cultured and civilized atmosphere. The town is full of pink and white houses, largely unspoilt; there is a handsome Town House with turreted tower, and Maclellan's Castle, really the town house of a Jacobean provost, right in the middle. A bit of old Greyfriars Kirk also survives, with the tomb of the said provost within. The Dee runs into the sea some miles to the south, this part of Galloway suffering like much of the Solway shore from sludgy low tides, a long way out. It is only when the water is high that one ventures to the harbour, or what was once the harbour at Kirkcudbright, and that any kind of boat can be induced to float.

The Galloway landscape was, I suppose, 'made' by Henry's picture of that title, the acknowledged masterpiece of the Glasgow School. It shows typical Gallovidian hillocks and bumpy Celtic fields with cows dotted about it – the cows, oddly enough, not 'Belties', black ones with a broad white stripe, or belt, which used to be characteristic but now seem almost to have disappeared. Besides the engagingly accidental scenery, the best parts a cross between Wales and Brittany, there is an air about Galloway which is difficult to define. It may be to do with the proximity of the sea, the marvellous colours in the hills and the relative remoteness of large towns. It is Highland in places but without the complete emptiness, with lochs and woods and fine houses. The highest hill is Merrick, nearly 3,000 feet above sea-level, from which, I am told, in clear weather one can see Scotland as far as the Highlands, Ireland, the Isle of Man, the English Lake District and even North Wales. The main snag about Galloway to my way of thinking is the single main road running the whole length of the country from Dumfries to Stranraer and the Irish ferries. As a road it is not bad, always interesting and wide enough for normal traffic, but when there are caravans and trailer-lorries on it, sometimes in number, one gets pretty fed up with the fumes and stour and the inability to pass. I suppose it would be worse if there was a motorway, though I am not sure. The old railway ran inland across the moors, bypassing the small towns whose isolated stations were often several miles away. It was a superb railway scenically, and constructionally, some of the viaducts now being maintained through the efforts of enthusiasts, while the last few miles have remained as a useful link between the south and Northern Ireland, the trains coming up from London nearly to Ayr, before turning down to the quayside at Stranraer.

My view really ends here, for one can go no further west nor nearly south in Scotland than Stranraer. Ireland can be glimpsed from the housetops and the atmosphere seems almost more Irish than Scots. Stranraer itself must have been nicer once, otherwise it would not have made its name as a holiday resort for North of England folk, but it is quickly losing its charm by over-commercialization and wholesale demolitions. One would almost think there was an oil boom or something causing all this, but no, it is the shuttle-service to and from Ulster plus the extra traffic caused by the present troubles across the Irish Sea. One looks straight out of Stranraer Harbour, down Loch Ryan, to that sea, just as one looks out from Dover towards France, but with perhaps more apprehension than anticipation here. One has to hold onto oneself to realize one is still in Scotland, the land of one's birth, in this far-away corner of it, as far south as County Durham, west of the Isle of Man and on a line with Milford Haven and Falmouth.

Western Galloway was, on the other hand, where Christianity first established itself in the north, in the days of the Roman Empire when St Ninian, a Romanized Briton, became our first bishop. He built his *Candida Casa*, or White House, at Whithorn, the base of which ancient cathedral has recently been identified under the ruins of a medieval successor. At Kirkmadrine I have seen carved stones with the insignia and names of three other early bishops, and it was by the same route, from Ulster via Galloway, that the message was relayed to Cumbria and through the Tyne gap to Northumberland and Yorkshire. It was an even older link than that forged by St Aidan and the Iona monks with Lindisfarne. The illuminated missals were transported this way for copying and on occasion to escape the ravages of the Danes: and curiously enough Galloway also witnessed the first stirrings of the Reformation, being visited by the followers of Wycliffe. Later it became a hotbed of Covenanting zealots,

The new parish kirk at Whithorn, from the kirkyard of the old priory, site of Scotland's first cathedral, St Ninian's Candida Casa, founded in the fifth century and dedicated to St Martin of Tours.

The view from a bedroom window in Lochnaw Castle, Stranraer. Seat of the Agnews since time immemorial, Lochnaw is within sight of Ulster, at the extreme south-western corner of Scotland.

when great cruelty and no mercy was shown by either side. The country is calm enough now, always beautiful and inspiring, except where the works of latter-day man, unmindful of posterity, break the spell and destroy the traditions of centuries.

The Mull of Galloway peninsula boasts the only place in Scotland where it never freezes and where snow is virtually unknown. St Patrick probably came from here; certainly he set sail for Ireland from what is now the small fishing-village of Portpatrick, and it is likely that he was the son of a Roman official. Inland are the Logan Gardens, full of tropical growths, and at Castle Kennedy is another semi-exotic garden, laid out originally by Lord Stair in the eighteenth century. He was ambassador at Versailles and much impressed by the formal arrangements there. Victorian descendants preferred the informality of an English park and changed the emphasis, making the old keep a folly and building for themselves a comfortable baronial mansion at Lochinch. None of this compares with the early-Christian memorials in the district, not even with Lochnaw Castle, which was built in the fifteenth century by an Agnew sheriff of the county, obviously with royal permission otherwise the date 1423 on a carved panel would be a fake. The Agnews, naturally, were of Norman extraction, the name deriving from the French for a lamb, and they have been at Lochnaw since time immemorial – that is, before the erection of the present castle, for there was an earlier fortress, possibly of wood, on an islet in the loch. The continuity was broken temporarily when a modern laird, suffering from anarchistic inclinations, decamped, and the castle became the home for a while of Sir Charles Hambro, who sold it to a Miss Agnew from Australia, so that Lochnaw is once again a family seat, though run as a trust and taking paying guests. It is filled with interesting furniture and houses a series of ancestral portraits on loan from the National Portrait Gallery in Edinburgh, a practice that ought to be more widely followed. The Victorians added an enormous extension to Lochnaw with an Irish-Gothic face which Sir Charles Hambro had the good sense to remove, and what we see today is the old fifteenth-century tower with Jacobean and Carolean adjuncts, which is modest enough to make restoration a viable proposition. The view, as expected, looks out over the loch towards Ireland, over a scene of deep greenness, with rhododendrons the size of trees, the rose-grey masonry of the castle making a wonderful contrast and at the same time recalling in its remoteness the Queen Mother's retreat at Mey, some 300 miles away as the crow flies. Here, however, one does not look beyond a protective walled garden to the cliffs of Orkney but across thick woods and water to a distant view of Antrim.

INDEX

Index